Camp Sharpe's "Psycho Boys"

From Gettysburg to Germany

Beverley Driver Eddy

Hoosick Falls, New York
2020

First Edition published in 2014 by the Merriam Press

Third Edition (2020)

ISBN 978-0-359-55778-3

Copyright © 2014 by Beverley Driver Eddy
Additional material copyright of named contributors.

All rights reserved.
No part of this book may be used or reproduced in any manner whatsoever without written permission, except in the case of brief quotations embodied in critical articles or reviews.

The unauthorized reproduction or distribution of this copyrighted work is illegal. Criminal copyright infringement, including infringement without monetary gain, is investigated by the FBI and is punishable by up to five years in federal prison and a fine of $250,000.

The views expressed are solely those of the author.

This work was designed, produced, and published in
the United States of America by the

Merriam Press
489 South Street
Hoosick Falls NY 12090

E-mail: ray@merriam-press.com
Web site: merriam-press.com

The Merriam Press has published numerous titles on historical subjects, especially military history, with an emphasis on World War II, as well as making available previously published works, including reports, documents, manuals, articles and other materials on historical topics, some in printed form with many as PDF files. Also the *World War II in Review* journal series and the *World War II Illustrated* pictorial series.

Contents

Introduction 5
Chapter 1: Founding Camp Sharpe 9
Chapter 2: Training and Leisure in Gettysburg 19
Chapter 3: Preparations in Britain 39
Chapter 4: The Struggle for France 57
Chapter 5: Luxembourg 81
Chapter 6: The Push into Germany 131
Chapter 7: Confronting the Camps 147
Chapter 8: Going "Home" 163
Chapter 9: Working for a Democratic Germany 175
Appendix: Members of the MRB Companies that Trained in Gettysburg ... 193
Bibliography 207
Index 215

Introduction

The "Psycho Boys" of Camp Sharpe were not your typical World War II soldiers. Most were not in particularly good physical shape, and many had trouble managing their weaponry. They differed widely in their ages, their political alliances, and their specialized skills. They were a strange blend of Americans and foreign nationals. All were fluent in at least two languages, and many were active in the arts. Their alumni include conservative journalist Victor Lasky, Communist Party activist Sarkis Phillian, Herzl Institute director Emil Lehman, railroad inspector Kenneth Hoag, German historian Hans Gatzke, brewery worker Michael Casiero, marketing genius Daniel Edelman, cookbook author Jules J. Bond, insurance salesman Roger Lajoie, foreign service officer Max Kraus, juvenile book illustrator Albert Orbaan, music critic Francis Perkins, restaurant owner Glenn Bernbaum, CIA officer Michael Josselson, radio personality Ralph Collier, and butterfly specialist Hans Epstein.

The U.S. Army sent these men—and about eight hundred others—to the historic town of Gettysburg, Pennsylvania, for specialized training in psychological warfare. There they were taught the various skills that would be necessary in the European campaign from D-Day onward: prisoner and civilian interrogation, broadcasting, loudspeaker appeals, leaflet and newspaper production, and technical support. These men were divided into four Mobile Radio Broadcasting (MRB) companies. They would, first, be employed in shortening the European war by lowering the morale of the enemy, then in easing the transition of Germany from a Nazi stronghold to an American-controlled democracy.

The army's air, artillery, and infantry men were highly skeptical of these psycho-warriors. At first many thought they were medics. They disapproved of the fact that their activities seemingly pulled Jeeps, tanks, planes, and shell casings away from active warfare. They were convinced that bombs and bullets, not bulletins, would bring about a speedy victory of the Allied forces and resented the fact that some of the activities of these "paragraphtroopers" brought the army's fighting men directly into the line of fire.

The men from Camp Sharpe eventually convinced many of the fighting forces that, although they did not kill Nazis, their activities resulted in hundreds, even thousands, of desertions from the enemy ranks. No detailed study has yet offered irrefutable proof of the degree of effectiveness of the "psycho boys'" various appeals to the German forces; it is probably impossible to do, since most of these activities were performed in concert with army and aircraft attacks. And yet anecdotal evidence suggests that these activities achieved very real and substantial results, in terms of the number of surrendering soldiers who came over with U.S. leaflets in their hands, in terms of testimony given by prisoners of war immediately after their capture, in terms of the audience size for the "pyscho boys'" broadcasts into both military and civilian zones. Despite the lack of concrete evidence, it is now generally accepted that the MRB men played a vital role as mediators between American and German forces, simply by telling the Germans the truth about the war and promising them fair treatment in the American prisoner of war camps and zones of occupation.

Because so many of the men from Camp Sharpe were active in academia, the arts, and media, there are a goodly number of reports about their individual activities in the war. Hanuš Burger, Igor Cassini, Ernst Cramer, Leon Edel, Albert Guerard, Hans Habe, Arthur Hadley, Stefan Heym, Walter Kohner, Si Lewen, and Peter Wyden wrote about their war-time experiences. Others—Arthur Bardos, Joseph Eaton, Curt Jellin, Samson Knoll, Gunter Kosse, Max Kraus, Fred Perutz, Albert Rosenberg, and Milton Stern—gave interviews in which they told of their activities as soldiers. These sources provide a multi-faceted picture of life at Camp Sharpe, the men's training in Gettysburg and in Great Britain, and their war and postwar activities in Europe, from the D-Day invasion of France through V-E Day and into the period of American military government in Germany.

In writing this book, I found that the three richest print resources for general information on the activities of the four MRB companies were the *History, Second Mobile Radio Broadcasting Company*, penned by its commanding officer, Captain Arthur H. Jaffe; *Fifth Mobile Radio Broadcasting Company*, penned by company member Clyde E. Shives; and the U.S. Army's *PWB Combat Team*, which outlines the course material presented to the soldiers at Gettysburg.

The two individuals who wrote in the greatest detail about the MRB companies' training in the States and their activities in Europe were Stefan Heym and Hanuš Burger. Unfortunately for American readers, these memoirs are available only in German. I have taken the liberty of translating numerous passages from them for inclusion in this study.

But the most compelling and, for me, most rewarding resources were those veterans of Camp Sharpe who are still alive and were willing to speak to me of their experiences. These men—Edward Alexander, Eddie Amicone, Harry Jacobs, Arthur Jaffe, Gunter Kosse, Si Lewen, Fred Perutz, Philip Pines, Albert Rosenberg, and Otto Schoeppler—not only provided much of the rich detail of this study; they were also able to answer my questions about materials that I found contradictory or confusing and to provide many of the photographs that appear in this book. Without their help, this book would have lacked many of the details that enliven this study.

There is, of course, a caveat implicit in all memoirs and oral interviews. Memories can be faulty, and the soldiers' stories might not always align properly with the facts of history. Sober historians write from a stance of skepticism and impartiality, while army veterans speak as individuals whose lives were directly impacted by war-time events. As a consequence, I have not set out to write a history of several World War II military propaganda units, but to create, instead, a collective biography of a group of men assigned with very specific tasks: preserving lives, winning German hearts and minds, soliciting information from Germans and liberated Europeans, providing the first newspapers and radio broadcasts for a conquered Germany, and working on the American de-Nazification program in the immediate aftermath of the war.

I have many people to thank for their contributions to this study, in addition to the veterans of the four MRB companies. Guy Stern called my attention to Camp Sharpe and stimulated my research into the men who trained there. Daniel Gross was immensely helpful; not only did he share with me his research into the personnel records of Camp Sharpe's four MRB companies, but he gave me the names and addresses of most of the veterans with whom I was able to gain interviews. Most importantly in this regard, he gave me the names of nearly all of the known MRB company members listed in the appendix to this work. Stephen Goodell was equally generous in searching out those photographs of the MRB units that are housed in the National Archives and Records Administration (NARA) and contributing a number of them to this study. Dan and Steve have both enriched my work immeasurably.

I would also like to thank Holly Fletcher for recovering articles from the *Gettysburg Times*, as well as the following people who donated material to this study: Edward Alexander, Helen Anger, Jon Groetzinger, Jr., Rainer Laabs, Jerry Lanson, Tami Lehman-Wilzig, Arthur McCardle, Bonita Ramsay, and Margret Schulze. Lydia Hecker, Document Delivery Specialist in the Inter-Library Loan Department of the Waidner-Spahr Library at Dickinson College, proved remarkably resourceful in helping me retrieve resources for this study, and I greatly appreciate her willingness to go the extra mile.

I am also grateful for the assistance given to me by librarians and staff of the following libraries: The U. S. Army Military History Institute in Carlisle (PA), the archives of the United States Holocaust Memorial Museum, the Jewish Federation of Greater Santa Barbara (CA), the Rauner Special Collections Library at Dartmouth College, the American Folklife Center of the Library of Congress, Brigham Young University's Harold B. Lee Library with its L. Tom Perry Special Collections, The USC Shoah Foundation Visual History Library, the Archibald S Alexander Library at Rutgers University, the Leo Baeck Institute, the library and research center at the Gettysburg National Military Park Museum and Visitor Center, and the archives of The Adams County Historical Society.

Finally, I must express my special gratitude to Christa Huss-Königsfeld and Catherine Ferguson for their encouragement, and to my husband Truman, without whose interest, advice, and steadfast support this project could never have been carried through to its successful completion.

Chapter 1

Founding Camp Sharpe

You get accustomed to a lot of things, in an army: the brain of the brass has its peculiar twists; but this had a stupid flavor all its own: placing men you want to send into future battles among the dead of a battle past!
Oh, Gettysburg![1]

On November 9, 1943, curious citizens of Gettysburg, Pennsylvania, might have noticed the arrival of a small band of U.S. Army men into that area of Gettysburg's "hallowed ground" now identified as "McMillan Woods." Many more army men were to follow in the weeks to come. The soldiers' mission was highly secret, but it soon became clear that the majority of these men were not your "typical" soldiers: many spoke English with a foreign accent, and a large percentage of the men were Jews. The first of these army men were receiving commando training in preparation to being sent behind German lines to gather intelligence, but they were soon followed by four specialized units called "Mobile Radio Broadcasting Companies," that were sent to Gettysburg for an intensive training program in psychological warfare and propaganda services. All would play a substantial role in the defeat of Germany.

The formation of these special forces had been a long time coming. Europe had been embroiled in war for more than two years before the Japanese attack on Pearl Harbor, but America had still entered the war ill prepared, both in terms of manpower and in the quality of its intelligence gathering.[2] American intelligence had been conducted internal-

---

[1] Stefan Heym, *The Lenz Papers*, 11.
[2] When, on September 15, 1940, President Franklin Roosevelt had signed into law the Selective Service and Training Act, which required all male citizens between the ages of 26 and 35 to register for the military draft, the total number of men in the American armed services (Army, Navy, and Marine Corps) was less than half a million, a number that, both out of military necessity and out of patriotism, would grow dramatically until, by the end of the war, it would reach over twelve million. These figures are taken from Infoplease, http://www.infoplease.com/ipa/A0004598.html

ly by the Federal Bureau of Investigation for many years, but foreign intelligence was lacking until Franklin Roosevelt appointed William J. Donovan Coordinator of Information in July, 1941. It was Donovan's task to gather and analyze intelligence information for the U.S. government's senior policymakers. In June 1942, this office was split into two civilian offices: the Office of War Information (OWI) and the Office of Strategic Services, or OSS, to coordinate U.S. espionage activities that, prior to that time, had been conducted on an ad-hoc basis by various governmental agencies.

The military, too, was slow to develop specialized intelligence training. The Army Air Corps had been the first to establish an intelligence training school; it was located in Harrisburg, Pennsylvania and opened in February 1942. And in June 1942 the Army opened a Military Intelligence Training Center at Fort Ritchie, Maryland, in what had formerly been a National Guard facility.

It was at Ritchie that the first Mobile Radio Broadcasting Company, or MRB company, had been formed for service in North Africa and in the Italian campaign. Under the command of Major Edward A. Caskey, this experimental psychological warfare unit arrived in North Africa in March 1943 and there joined forces with British propaganda experts in a highly successful campaign that proved that psychological warfare was "one of the most important supporting weapons of modern warfare."[3] In Africa, and later in Sicily and in continental Italy, men of the First Mobile Radio Broadcasting Company interrogated war prisoners about German troop movement and morale, wrote and distributed propaganda leaflets across enemy lines, broadcast to the enemy, and made loudspeaker appeals to German troops to surrender. A young British officer, Captain Con O'Neill, made a great advancement in propaganda warfare during this time by inventing a technique for distributing leaflets into enemy territory by artillery shells, a move that "revolutionized the dissemination of combat propaganda" and made it possible for the American and British combat teams to distribute leaflets and, later, even a German-language newspaper directly into the enemy front lines.[4] As a result of these activities in psychological warfare, an entire German regiment in Tunisia surrendered to a written appeal.[5]

---

[3] Edward A. Caskey, "Introduction," *PWB Combat Team...*, 5.
[4] Edward A. Caskey, "Introduction," *PWB Combat Team...*, 3.
[5] Edward A. Caskey, "Introduction," *PWB Combat Team...*, 2.

General Dwight David Eisenhower was one of the few American wartime leaders who bought wholeheartedly into the concept of coordinated wartime intelligence activities as an important part of the Allied war effort. In North Africa and in Italy this had been done through the Psychological Warfare Branch (PWB) of the Allied Force Headquarters. This became the model for the Psychological Warfare Division (PWD) of the Supreme Headquarters Allied Expeditionary Force (SHAEF) that prepared for the invasion of mainland Europe across the British channel in June 1944. The 1st Mobile Radio Broadcasting Company, then, had acted under the Allied Force Headquarters; the 2nd, 3rd, 4th and 5th would be acting under SHAEF.[6]

As part of the preparations for the invasion of France, a 32-year-old lieutenant named Hans Habe was recalled from his assignment with the 1st MRB company to Washington, D.C., where he was assigned the task of assisting in the training of four more MRB companies.

Hans Habe was an extremely colorful—some would say controversial—figure. He was a Hungarian by birth and a newspaperman by trade. Even before America's entry into the war, he had proved his abilities on the battlefield as a volunteer in the French foreign legion. He had been captured, imprisoned, and later, with the help of French friends, he had escaped from the Dieuze Dulag, or transit prison camp, in Lorraine, France. He had emigrated to America, quickly become an American citizen, and turned his prison camp experiences into a best-selling novel called *A Thousand Shall Fall* (*Ob Tausende fallen*, 1941). Two years later, this novel formed the basis for the Hollywood film *The Cross of Lorraine*, featuring Jean-Pierre Aumont, Gene Kelly, Peter Lorre, and Hume Cronyn. In 1942, Habe married Eleanor Post Hutton, heiress of General Foods; it was his third marriage, her fourth. Eleanor Post Hutton's stepfather, Joseph Davies, had served as American ambassador to the Soviet Union from 1937 to 1938. Through the spectacular success of his novel, the wealth of his wife, and the political clout of his new father-in-law, Habe became a prominent figure in the Washington social scene. When his wife gave birth to their son, Anthony Niklas Habe, Eleanor Roosevelt served as godmother.

---

[6] Most of this information is taken from: Frank Prosser and SGM Herbert A. Friedman (Ret.), "Organization of the United States Propaganda Effort During World War II."

During his tour of duty with the 1st MRB company, Habe had proven remarkably adept both at questioning war prisoners and in composing effective propaganda pamphlets. Now it was his task to develop these skills in four new companies of soldiers.

At Habe's meeting with his superiors in Washington D.C., it was determined that these skills should be developed in greater secrecy at a Fort Ritchie sub-camp devoted strictly to psychological warfare. As one of the members of the 2nd MRB company, a Czech filmmaker named Hanuš Burger[7], would tell it, Gettysburg, Pennsylvania's "admittedly somewhat decaying Camp Sharpe" became Habe's "sandbox," given him to do exactly as he wished, "because here at last someone had come who apparently was willing to take this job upon himself."[8] As Habe put it,

> I was [...] to train four companies for the landing in France. [...] As the man in charge of the training [...], I was furnished with full powers that many a general might have envied. I was allowed to pick from the superbly organized card indexes of the War Department those men whom I considered suitable for the task in hand, and within forty-eight hours the people thus chosen would arrive at Gettysburg.[9]

Until November 1943, the camp on the edge of the Gettysburg Battlefield was known only as CCC Gettysburg 2; it had housed an all-Black unit of Civilian Conservation Corps members brought in to clear the battlefield of brush, build bridges, roads, and outbuildings, and in general beautify the battlefield before and after the 1938 Civil War veterans' reunion and the dedication of the Peace Light monument at the north end of town. The corps quarters had been vacated in March, 1942. In November, 1943, the Gettysburg papers reported that the abandoned camp had been converted into a small army camp, because of "the expansion at the regular camp site and in connection with extensive training activities instituted by the main encampment." The

---

[7] His official war documents list him as Hans Herbert Burger, and he is more widely known in the United States as Hans Burger. Burger was a Communist and sometime courier for the Czech Communist Party. He left Czechoslovakia after the 1938 Nazi takeover of the country.

[8] Hanuš Burger, *Der Frühling war es wert*, 143-144. All translations from this volume are my own.

[9] Hans Habe, *All My Sins*, 341, 342.

main encampment, Ritchie, was not named, but the association was indicated by the statement that "The local camp, a temporary setup, has been named Camp George H. Sharpe in memory of General George Gordon Meade's Intelligence Officer during the Battle of Gettysburg."[10]

Clearly, the camp's mission must involve intelligence gathering. Clearly the mission was secret. The camp was, in fact, "surrounded by such secrecy that it was not even connected by telephone."[11] No one, even at Camp Ritchie, was to be informed of what was going on at Gettysburg.

The first men to come to Gettysburg were not part of Habe's training program, however; they were men who had already completed their course work in military intelligence at Camp Ritchie and were now being sent to Gettysburg for intensive combat training in a separate, more isolated locale. Gunter Kosse was one of these men; he was a German Jew who had grown up in Berlin. At age sixteen, he had emigrated to Cuba. At the time he was called up for military service, he was nineteen years old, living in New York with his parents, and working as an apprentice diamond cutter.

Kosse had already completed ten months of training at Camp Ritchie before being assigned to Gettysburg. He recalls that Charles M. Banfield, the commandant at Camp Ritchie, had told the army that his men could perform any task required of them, but that they would need Ranger (i.e., commando) training if they were to be sent behind enemy lines to gather information. These missions behind enemy lines were called "cattle alerts" and required, in addition to intelligence training, special physical skills. As a result, about sixty of those Ritchie men who had already completed their coursework and participated in maneuvers[12] were called out one day and told that they should pack their basic equipment, take their weapons, and prepare for a twenty-mile march. In typical fashion, whenever a Ranger unit set off on a strenuous march, they were followed by an ambulance. But on the

---

[10] "Temporary Army Camp on 'Field'," *Gettysburg Compiler*, 13 Nov. 1943.
[11] Habe, *All My Sins*, 342.
[12] Gunter Kosse had participated in maneuver training in Camp Young, California, where the Mojave Desert doubled for North Africa; after the closing of this camp, he had been sent from Camp Ritchie to Lebanon, Tennessee. Author interview with Gunter Kosse, 18 Jan. 2014.

march to Gettysburg, not one of the men fell out.[13] Commando training went far beyond the normal military exercises of the average GI. Gunter Kosse remembers that, when they first came to Gettysburg, the camp had not yet been named; it was still known only as a CCC camp. They arrived in November, but there was already snow on the ground. At the camp, they lived the rough life of Rangers, eating from mess kits and sleeping on folding field cots.

They were given strenuous physical training, which took advantage of the battlefield in all kinds of weather. Often there were forced marches at night, meaning that the men had to travel seven miles an hour while laden with heavy field equipment. Private Kosse was struck by the strange beauty of these nighttime marches, illuminated only by moonlight, among the statues of Civil War soldiers and generals. The men also did extended ordered drill: these were little infantry maneuvers in which they practiced jumping into and out of fox holes and storming hills. As part of their weapons and bayonet training, the men learned how to take apart machine guns and put them back together under the worst of conditions: when the guns were frozen, for example, and while the men were blindfolded.[14]

After some weeks, the men were shipped off on an English ship to Northern Ireland for further training in Donaghadee, and the 2nd MRB company took their places in the barracks of what was now known to everyone as Camp Sharpe. Hans Habe personally selected twenty-two men from those stationed at Camp Ritchie as the heart of his 2nd MRB company. Indeed, many of those eventually selected for the four MRB companies would go through some training at Camp Ritchie before transferring to Sharpe; others, with greater experience, would be directly reassigned to Sharpe from other locations and other duties. German-born Lieutenant Albert Rosenberg, for example, had already served in the U.S. Army as a meteorologist in Brazil, then trained as an officer in tank warfare in Kentucky before being called to Sharpe.[15]

---

[13] Not all those who participated in this program were as fortunate. Harry Jacobs was sent, with a smaller group of ca. 20 potential rangers, on the same march to Gettysburg in December, 1943; his feet froze and, after two or three days, he had to be sent back to Camp Ritchie to be hospitalized. Author interview with Harry Jacobs, 2 Oct. 2013.

[14] Author interviews with Gunter Kosse, 23 Sept. and 9 Oct. 2013.

[15] Albert G. Rosenberg was born in Göttingen, and was studying at the university in that town when he was savagely beaten by Nazi storm troopers.

continued...

Novelist/critic Albert Guerard[16] was called away from Ann Arbor, Michigan, where the army had sent him to learn Japanese. Sergeant Phil Pinkofsky[17], a Brooklyn native and a graduate student in Columbia University's history department, had already been trained by the Army as a radio engineer, then assigned to the 111th Infantry Regiment; he was operating radios at Camp Ashby in Virginia when he and two of his fellow soldiers there were called up to Gettysburg.[18] With an eye to the transition to a post-war Europe, the army had originally assigned Viennese-born Fred Perutz[19] to a uniquely "Austrian" battalion, but this had to be disbanded when unhappy political factions, including those "non-Austrians" who had been born in the old Austro-Hungarian Empire, rebelled and refused to wear the "Free Austria" shoulder patch.[20] Perutz then became part of the 4th MRB; he also served as one of a team of four sent to universities across America to interview soldiers interested in joining the 5th MRB. As part of the interview process the team paid particular attention to the new recruits' abilities in French and German.[21] As one of those interviewees, Edward Alexander[22] applied to the MRBs from the U.S. Army Signal Corps; he was sent to Boston University for an intensive crash course in German before his transfer to Gettysburg.[23] As one company histo-

---

...continued

He was able to gain entry into the United States in 1937 and was studying at the University of Miami School of Law when drafted into the U.S. Army.

[16] Albert J. Guerard was born in Houston, Texas. He earned his doctorate in English literature from Stanford University and was teaching at Harvard at the time of his enlistment.

[17] After the war, Pinkofsky changed his name to Pines. I will refer to him as "Pines" rather than "Pinkofsky" in the remainder of this study.

[18] Author interview with Philip Pines, 15 Aug. 2013.

[19] For two generations the Perutz family had operated a raw cotton import business in Vienna. A relative in New York sent the family affidavits that made it possible for them to come to the United States in April, 1938; Fred spent most of the next years in Waco, Texas, as an apprentice in the cotton business before entering the U.S. Army in 1943.

[20] See Syd Jones, "Austrian Americans."

[21] Author interview with Fred Perutz, 28 Sept. 2013.

[22] Edward Alexander was born in New York city of Armenian parents. He had earned a Master of Science degree from Columbia University's Graduate School of Journalism prior to his enlistment.

[23] Author interview with Edward Alexander, 21 June 2013.

rian put it, "dozens of radio technicians, German-speaking personnel and drivers began to pour in from camps throughout the country."[24]

Everyone, from the average doughboy to commanding officers to the company members themselves, would agree that the men of the MRB companies were an unusual lot. The German writer Stefan Heym, for example, was the author of the best-selling novel *Hostages,* that had recently been made into a Hollywood film; Boris Kremenliev was a Bulgarian-born composer and musicologist with a PhD from the Eastman School of Music; the Czech author Joseph Wechsberg was a columnist for *The New Yorker* and "an authority on gastronomic matters";[25] Cleveland-born Tony Strobl was a Disney artist who had worked on *Fantasia, Pinocchio,* and *Dumbo*; the Russian-born count Igor Cassini was a prominent gossip columnist; Walter Kohner and Fred Lorenz[26] (Manfred Inger) had been successful stage actors in Austria.[27] Among the members of the 2nd Mobile Radio Broadcasting Company—143 men and 21 officers—thirty-three languages were spoken—although German and French were dominant.[28] The regular Army, in fact, would refer to the men of the MRBs as a "unit of geniuses."[29] Because of the high percentage of Jews in training there, the men stationed at Camp Sharpe jokingly referred to it as "Camp Shapiro."[30]

When the first full contingent of MRB men arrived at the camp, it consisted of four barracks for enlisted men (sleeping quarters and classrooms), and one for officers; company and battalion headquarters; housing for the battalion CO; a sparsely furnished recreation hall; a supply building; mess hall; showers; latrine; and an extensive motor pool area with garages, two workshops and dispatch office. Later on, a

---

[24] [Clyde Shives] "History of the Fifth," *Fifth Mobile Radio Broadcasting Company.*
[25] Habe, *All My Sins*, 342.
[26] Before his emigration to the United States, Fred Lorenz' name was Manfred Inger, a name that he resumed when he returned to Vienna in 1949.
[27] Daniel Gross has estimated that, among the four MRB companies that trained in Gettysburg, 38% were foreign born and 21% were born in Germany or Austria.
[28] Interview with Arthur Jaffe, 11 July, 2013.
[29] Habe, *All My Sins*, 342.
[30] See Peter Wyden, "Die bunte Truppe von Camp Shapiro."

training platoon of army engineers, mostly Mohawk Indians, would erect an 80-foot antenna tower on the grounds.[31]

As one of the first of the MRB transferees into Gettysburg, the Henry James scholar Leon Edel[32] expressed his dismay upon arriving at Camp Sharpe on January 3rd, 1944: "After an hour we stopped. We were [...] a mere fifty miles [sic] from Ritchie, parked in a muddy hollow at the bottom of a slanting road, just outside the national park of Gettysburg. The barracks [...] were filled with dust and cobwebs. The windows looked as if mud had been smeared across them. Mice and rats had left their deposits."[33] Edel hastened to throw his duffel bag onto an upper bunk to lay claim to what he hoped were slightly protected sleeping quarters.

The MRB men did not adjust as easily as the Rangers had to the harsh living conditions at Camp Sharpe. Both the officers and the trainees agreed that, after the relative luxury of Camp Ritchie, life at Sharpe was "rugged and barren." The novelist Stefan Heym found the barracks to be more like hovels ("Schuppen") than dwellings, "in different stages of scantily painted-over decay."[34] The barracks were "surrounded by a sea of mud," the wind "whistled through gaps in the walls[,] while four stoves tried in vain to keep up the room temperature."[35] The novelist-critic Albert Guerard fell into momentary disfavor when he neglected his duty one night of keeping the stoves burning in his barracks. Officers were not allowed to live together with their wives at the camp, as they had at Ritchie. The only exception that anyone was aware of was one weekend when Hans Habe's wife broke the strict camp regulations and spent the night on the Camp Sharpe grounds.[36]

Major John T. Jarecki was the camp commander. He was a lawyer in civilian life and had graduated with the Fifth Class at Fort Ritchie, where he had specialized in photo interpretation. Arthur Jaffe, a lieutenant at Sharpe and, later, captain and commander of the 2nd MRB

---

[31] Interview with Si Lewen, 26 July 2013.
[32] Leon Edel was a true cosmopolitan. Although born in Pittsburgh, he was raised in Saskatchewan, Canada. He studied at McGill University in Montreal, and earned his doctorate at the Sorbonne in Paris.
[33] Leon Edel, *The Visitable Past*, 22
[34] Stefan Heym, *Nachruf*, 261. All translations from this work are my own.
[35] [Jaffe] , History, p. 20.
[36] Interview with Si Lewen, 26 July 2013.

company[37], remembers Jarecki as a "good detail man."[38] Still, it was Lieutenant Habe who dictated the program to be taught to the soldiers in the elite propaganda units. It was he who first interviewed each soldier selected for these units and it was he who assigned them to specific areas of concentration. These assignments were made sometime during the first week of classes. The artist Si Lewen[39] recalls that Habe selected Prussians for broadcasting, because he "thought the Prussian accent carried weight." He told Lewen that he would "work well as an interpreter."[40]

The men trained in broadcasting would eventually be assigned either to "white" or "black" radio work. The white broadcasts would be those admittedly made by Americans, while those making "black" broadcasts would pretend to be Germans loyal to the Fuehrer. For white broadcasts in German, an American accent was acceptable, and sometimes even desired. Those who spoke perfect "Prussian" German could be used for both types of broadcasting.

After these and similar placements, the company personnel were organized into sections: headquarters, radio, propaganda, printing, and motor pool.[41] The men's training at Sharpe would last from one week to three months, depending on their previous training and experience.

---

[37] Arthur H. Jaffe was a native of Butler, Pennsylvania. Because of his fine singing voice, he had had some training as a cantor. Prior to entering the army, he attended Pennsylvania State University, where he majored in Classical Greek.

[38] Author interview with Arthur Jaffe, 1 Aug. 2013. After his duties at Camp Sharpe ended, Jarecki was assigned to the legal department of the Signal Corps, where he assisted in the reorganization of Radio Tokyo.

[39] Officially, Lewen's name was "Simon Lewin"; "Lewen" was his artist's name. He was born in Lublin, Poland, but, when he was a child, he and his family fled to Germany to escape the violence of ethnic pogroms. Later, when he was 14, he and his older brother fled to France and then to America to escape the Nazis. The family joined them there in 1935. Lewen was taking art classes in New York City when America entered the war.

[40] Interview with Si Lewen, 26 July 2013.

[41] [Clyde Shives], "History of the Fifth," *Fifth Mobile Radio Broadcasting Company*.

Chapter 2

Training and Leisure in Gettysburg

> *As training proceeded, the separate sections soon became "expert" in their jobs. When the radio men disappeared inside their "rigs," they unraveled many of the mysteries of their equipment. Our printing section, all of whom were skilled craftsmen, were getting the feel of their mobile equipment and growing accustomed to working in confined quarters; while the propaganda section attended classes under the direction of [...] Hans W. Habe, who taught the use of psychological warfare's weapons: the controlled dissemination of news, facts and ideas. The motor pool bristled with activity[,] for they were busily engaged in the never-ending, unsung task of maintenance and care of the [company's] vehicles, which ranged from the lowly jeep to the huge ten ton semi-trailers.*[42]

Most of the company's authors, professors, actors, and filmmakers were assigned to the propaganda section. Here all the men trained for a variety of assignments: some might be sent to film or take photographs in the battle zones, for purposes of propaganda; some would broadcast in different languages, to local populations as well as to the German army; some would serve as translators and interpreters; some would interrogate prisoners and civilians; some would monitor German and civilian radio and newspapers in order to gather information and gauge morale; some would produce posters and leaflets in record time for the changing war conditions. Despite this possibility of future specialization, all were to be instructed in all techniques of propaganda. And Hans Habe was the main instructor.

Classes were held in the barracks furthest to the rear of the camp; this had been set up with brand new desks and a large blackboard next to the teacher's table, and the soldiers were each given a supply of fresh notebooks and pencils. As the men sat there, waiting for something to happen, suddenly "someone appears, like a comet, sparkling, glides

---

[42] [Clyde Shives], "History of the Fifth," *5th Mobile Radio Broadcasting Company*.

past them, along the center aisle, stops before the blackboard, turns slowly towards the men, who are watching him in astonishment, and informs them who he is, First Lieutenant Hans Habe de Bekessy,[43] returned from Africa."[44] The men were all amazed—and amused—by Habe's appearance. Contrary to army regulations, Habe's hair was dyed chestnut-brown, with blond tints (in Europe the regular army officers would call him "Goldilocks").[45] Edward Alexander recalls that Habe not only dyed his hair, but rouged his cheeks, as well.[46] He wore a gold cross around his neck. "When he ran his fingers through [his hair], several gold rings flashed. There was something old-fashioned about this foppish man, who had an absent, far-away look in his gray eyes."[47]

In addition, Habe was "undoubtedly the best-dressed officer in the U.S. Army."[48] Stefan Heym[49] remarked that, "in the United States Army, only generals were permitted to wear special uniforms tailored according to their taste—and Lieutenant Habe."[50] Each day Habe followed the same pattern of entering the classroom from the rear, walking to the front of the room, pausing in front of the blackboard, and then swinging around to face his students. The ritual was deliberate: despite his heroism on the battlefield and his brilliance as an interrogator, he was, at heart, an actor and fop.[51] Otto Schoeppler found him "both vain and conceited." He remembers him "as never being in a regular uniform—but in riding boots, jodhpurs and a leather vest."[52] But Habe had a way of making even a regulation uniform uniquely his own, "be it the hue of his jacket or the interplay in the combination of

---

[43] "Habe" was an adopted name, based on the German pronunciation of "H.B."—Bekessy's initials. He was not nobility, despite the "de" that he added to his real last name.
[44] Stefan Heym, *Nachruf*, 264.
[45] Hanuš Burger, *Der Frühling war es wert*, 144.
[46] Interview with Edward Alexander, 21 June 2013.
[47] Leon Edel, *The Visitable Past*, 23.
[48] Hanuš Burger, *Der Frühling war es wert*, 141.
[49] Stefan Heym was born Helmut Flieg, in Czernowitz, Bukovina (now Ukraine). He was studying in Berlin when Hitler came to power. He fled to Prague and contributed to Communist periodicals there. In 1935 he was offered a scholarship by a Jewish fraternity at the University of Chicago, and moved to the United States.
[50] Stefan Heym, *Nachruf*, 264.
[51] Interview with Edward Alexander, 21 June 2013.
[52] Letter to the author from Otto Schoeppler, 18 Aug. 2013.

light and dark in his shirt and tie, field blouse and breeches."[53] Habe himself admitted to vanity in his dress; in the French army, he had "attached particular importance to looking like a stage soldier amid the filthy hell of Barcarès,"[54] and, while in prison camp, had, "though my stomach was rumbling, traded [two loaves of bread] for an almost new sergeant's uniform."[55] Leon Edel recalls that Habe also accessorized his uniform: "Sartorially, Habe seemed determined to get away from army monotony. A white silk handkerchief hung out of his breast pocket; he wore a jeweled tiepin in his regulation necktie. A watch chain was visible when he unbuttoned his jacket."[56] Peter Weidenreich[57] added: "It was like perpetually being at a show, at a circus just to see this guy perform. I would have paid money for it"[58]

Even before he was assigned to an MRB company, gossip columnist Igor Cassini[59] had mocked Habe's flamboyantly aristocratic airs in the Washington papers, noting that he slept "in black silk sheets, as any Don Juan writer should."[60]

Leon Edel was particularly amused by Habe's speech:

> Once he started describing the nature of psychological warfare, he revealed a strange mix of Anglo-French words and expressions. "I'm here," he said, "to tell you some dopes." He

---

[53] Stefan Heym, *Nachruf*, 264.
[54] Hans Habe, *All My Sins*, 247.
[55] Hans Habe, *All My Sins*, 263.
[56] Leon Edel, *The Visitable Past*, 22-23.
[57] After the war, Weidenreich changed his name to "Wyden." I will use "Wyden" throughout this study. He was a German Jew, born in Berlin. He left Nazi Germany and came to New York City in 1937, when he was thirteen. Prior to the war he studied at City University of New York.
[58] Cited in Jessica Gienow-Hecht, *Transmission Impossible*, 21.
[59] Igor Cassini was born in Sevastopol, Russia (now Ukraine), to a Russian diplomat father and an Italian-Russian aristocrat mother. When the family lost its fortune in the wake of the Russian Revolution of 1917, the family moved to Italy, where he was raised before moving to the U.S. with his family in 1936. He achieved national notoriety in 1939 when he was kidnapped, tarred and feathered because of a society column he had written in a Virginia newspaper. He was extremely popular among his fellow soldiers at Sharpe, although all agreed that he was not cut out for the military life. Because of Cassini's Russian and Italian background, Hans Habe was skeptical about his loyalties.
[60] Igor Cassini, *I'd do it all over again*, 97.

spoke of "changement" and "groupment." He told us "how many innumerable" things he had to cover. He was forced to "condensate." Having condensated, he offered "a few additional datas."[61]

Stefan Heym recalled, that "Habe's manner of speaking was fascinating; his somewhat squawking, nasal voice did not allow his listeners to shut down, however tired they were, and the powerful gaze of those large, bright, slightly protruding eyes always seemed to demand some reaction to his assessments, desires, and challenges."[62]

In spite of his foppishness and his unusual manner of speaking, Habe was an effective instructor who won the grudging admiration of the worst skeptics:

> He was amazing. Not only did he slip with no apparent difficulty from one role to another—it would not have surprised us, if he had changed clothes and makeup in every one of our short breaks like a quick change artist in a vaudeville theater. He was by turns German teacher, journalist, radio director, political lecturer, copy editor, language teacher, voice trainer, psychology professor—whatever the course material required.[63]

This was all the more remarkable in that "in these moldy, cold November barracks we were, even in political respects, a motley bunch of people—Communists, Sympathizers, Anti-Communists. Habe managed to bind us together for our assigned task."[64] Stefan Heym, whose own socialist political views could not have been further from Habe's, noted:

> I know no one in the American army, except for a few extroverted generals like MacArthur or Patton, about whom people gossiped with such relish as Lieutenant, later Captain, later Major Hans Habe. But I also know no one whose individual contribution to the development of psychological warfare in this army contributed so much to its victory. [...] Be-

---

[61] Leon Edel, *The Visitable Past*, 23.
[62] Stefan Heym, *Nachruf*, 264.
[63] Hanuš Burger, *Der Frühling war es wert*, 144.
[64] Hanuš Burger, *Der Frühling war es wert*, 144.

neath all the flickering and all the glitz stood a man of industry, great knowledge, and, occasionally, heart.[65]

Lieutenant Albert Rosenberg (4th MRB company) agreed: "He was highly intelligent, a very creative-thinking person with a remarkable sense of humor."[66]

The emphasis throughout this training was on policies that had been worked out with British military intelligence. The mission of the Sharpe boys would be two-fold: first of all,

> to get the Germans [...] to believe in what they were being told by the U.S. and by the British, and second, to get the Germans to question their regime. [...] We had to focus on inconsistencies in German policies from the point of view of the German public and the differentiation between what was good for the general public, and what was good [...] for the maintenance of the regime.[67]

This was not to be "the Hollywood approach [...], in which you often times make claims that are [...] misleading."[68] Ever since Dunkirk, when British intelligence decided to tell the truth about Britain's horrific losses, the BBC had gained authority throughout Europe as an objective source of news. The Sharpe boys were now to be trained to do the same.

Fifty-minute classes—with ten minute breaks between them—were held each day from nine until five. One set of lectures was on interrogation. Habe treated this extensively, including such issues as timing, settings, and estimating prisoner vulnerability. He said it was usually good to interrogate prisoners within five to ten hours of capture, because the prisoner then reflected most accurately the morale of the comrades he had left behind. He stressed the importance of making the place of interrogation look impressive to the prisoners, by creating "at least the semblance of an office." The interrogator "must command

---

[65] Stefan Heym, *Nachruf*, 265.
[66] Author interview with Albert Rosenberg, 6 Jan. 2014.
[67] Interview with Joseph Eaton by Judith Cohen, United States Holocaust Memorial Museum, 1 Aug. 2010, 36.
[68] Interview with Joseph Eaton by Judith Cohen, United States Holocaust Memorial Museum, 1 Aug. 2010, 35.

respect. [...] Headgear [must] be worn when the prisoner enters and leaves" the interrogation area, because "the German soldier is not familiar with salutes rendered while uncovered." He taught the Sharpe soldiers how to evaluate whether a prisoner was going to be "tough" or "easy" to crack. As a rule of thumb, the "easiest" prisoners were, first, "Poles, then Yugoslavs, then Germans; enlisted men, then noncommissioned officers, then officers." [69] But there were frequently exceptions to this. Interrogators must be patient, and develop techniques for determining who, among the German prisoners, would likely be "tough" or "easy":

> A good question to this end is: "How long do you think you are going to be a P.W.?" A "tough" prisoner will usually give a defiant answer, such as "Until the war is over." If he answers, "I don't know," he is likely to prove an "easy" prisoner, and you may follow by asking: "Do you think you will be sent back to Germany right after the war?" If his answer is yes, he believes in German victory; if no, he has admitted by implication his belief that Germany will lose the war. A good method of "warming up" a "tough" prisoner is to ask him how he was captured[,] because it affords him an opportunity for self-justification. For an "easy" prisoner, simple "warming up" questions such as "What part of Germany are you from?" or "How old are you?" are adequate.[70]

Habe taught the men various psychological techniques that were effective when questioning difficult German officers. He suggested that interrogators first ask a few military questions to which they already knew the answers:

> This will give the prisoner the satisfaction of refusal. You will then supply the answers yourself, thereby showing your knowledge and easing his mind on the point of military security. [...] [T]he officer will feel that this military information is the real objective of your interrogation [...]. From this point on the interrogation may turn to the not strictly "military" subjects [that] you are really interested in and the significance

---

[69] *PWB Combat Team...*, 27.
[70] *PWB Combat Team...*, 28-29.

of which German officers rarely appreciate.[71]

At the end of the lectures, the Camp Sharpe participants were then called upon to do practice interrogations under the watchful eye of Habe and their classmates, who then critiqued their performances.

Another important part of the training at Camp Sharpe was radio monitoring. "The monitor is a news reporter," Habe told the men. "It is his job to listen to news broadcasts and to report them as faithfully as possible. [...] He must train himself to listen patiently and to record quickly and accurately what he hears."[72] Since most of the men did not know shorthand, Habe taught them a "cue word system" to use in its place. This involved a system of word abbreviations that the men could then expand and work into complete sentences when the broadcast was over. As an example, Habe read the cue word notes from a radio monitor serving in the 1st MRB in Italy: "5 AR 8 AR JN 10 M SE VAL ON VIA CAS," showing how, after the broadcast, the monitor was able to fill this cryptic passage out, so that it read: "A JUNCTION BETWEEN THE 5th AND 8th ARMIES WAS EFFECTED TEN MILES SOUTHEAST OF VALMONTONE, ALONG THE VIA CASILINA."[73]

It was necessary for the men to have complete mastery of personal and geographic names as well as cue words in order to be effective monitors. Their work had to be accurate; monitors were not to editorialize, but to make their reports as comprehensive as they were able. Habe told his student monitors: "Don't strive for style or color. Stick to the facts, write them simply and clearly."[74] They were not to skip any news items, however unimportant they might appear. The chief monitor would then arrange the monitors' reports, by classifying them as "Allied," "Enemy" or "Neutral" news stories; then he would index them and write a page of "Personalities in the News" and another of "Highlights in the News." These reports would be mimeographed and distributed to all the men on their team working as writers for print or radio.

Many of the Sharpe soldiers found monitoring radio broadcasts to be one of their most difficult tasks; it was much easier to monitor for-

---

[71] *PWB Combat Team...*, 29.
[72] *PWB Combat Team...*, 35.
[73] *PWB Combat Team...*, 36.
[74] *PWB Combat Team...*, 36.

eign language reports available in print medium (newspapers, magazines, posters, etc.). All in the propaganda division were required to take several turns at preparing a report based on the news broadcasts available to them in Gettysburg.

They also learned how to use the chief monitor's reports in other propaganda venues. For example, broadcasting teams, each made up of an editor, script writers, announcers, and producer, learned how to prepare news programs based on monitor reports. The scriptwriters rewrote them to make them suitable for 15-minute broadcast news segments. They were trained to keep their sentences short, use adjectives sparingly, and keep the language simple. They rounded out their news reports with feature pieces: these might be educational in nature, a surrender appeal, a description of the P.W. camps, or simply a "hot" topic of the day. They were frequently produced with music, several voices, a dialogue or interview. Personal interest pieces could be written to appeal to German civilians. Habe taught the men an interesting technique for holding the interest of German audiences: at the beginning of a feature story, the announcer could give the names of prisoners in U.S. camps in a somewhat muffled voice, while mentioning that these names would be repeated at the end. This device would keep listeners glued to the radio until the end of the broadcast, when the names would be repeated quite clearly and the listeners could hear whether or not friends or family members were among those listed.

The Sharpe students had to take turns doing these and other tasks, and were subjected to sharp criticism by their fellow students and by Habe. Hanuš Burger[75] has commented that "it was a hands-on training course, like I had never experienced before. The lesson resembled that of a higher journalism academy."[76] In print, as in broadcasting, everyone was trained in all aspects of text preparation: writing, style, and layout.

---

[75] Hanuš Burger was born in Prague to German-Jewish parents. He studied in Frankfurt and was involved in theater in Hamburg until 1931, when the worsening political situation in Germany drove him back to Prague, where he continued his work in the theater. There he and the fugitive Stefan Heym became acquainted and collaborated on the drama *Tom Sawyer's Great Adventure* (*Tom Sawyers grosses Abenteuer*). He was hired by an American journalist to make a documentary film about the condition in German-occupied Czechoslovakia; this led to his move to New York, where he continued his work as a documentary film maker.

[76] Hanuš Burger, *Der Frühling war es wert*, 142.

As in broadcasting, work with print material began with the information given in the chief monitor's daily reports. Habe emphasized, again and again, that in writing stories, whether for broadcasting or for print, "one main idea should carry through the feature."[77] Years later, the German political scientist Konrad Kellen (2nd MRB company) would recall how Habe used to ask, whenever someone sought permission to print a poster or propaganda leaflet: "Where is the red thread?"[78]

The men learned that their propaganda leaflets would be printed on small sheets of paper so that they could be fired in artillery shells across German lines. The point was to encourage the German troops to surrender. The sheets should emphasize the good treatment that prisoners received in the American camps, the adherence there to the terms of the Geneva Convention, the promise that they could communicate with their families by mail, and assurances that they would be returned home at the end of the war. These assurances were generally printed on the backside of the leaflets, along with instructions on how to surrender; the front sides should aim, as a rule, to be more "sober and terrifying," and yet be "simple but striking enough to have souvenir value." These "striking" pages were, as a rule, tactical in nature, and written to address a specific combat situation. Habe noted that, "Enemy soldiers have often kept a leaflet on this basis, not using it immediately, but under the pressure of later military events coming to present it as a means of entry into our lines."[79]

Before the Sharpe students composed their own leaflets, they were given examples to study and critique. One of these "unsatisfactory" examples contained 36 different violations of the principles of good propaganda. It began with the heading, "How much longer?" (wrong; one must not show impatience), and then read "Tomorrow, at 7.31, (one must never prophesy) the Sixth Parachute regiment will disappear from the earth (one must avoid bombastic language). We have heard from one German prisoner (one must never use information obtained from fewer than eight, and one must say "Prisoner of war," not "German prisoner") that you have received insufficient nourishment (one must not mention discomforts suffered by all soldiers)."[80] And so on.

Habe applied these same principles for leaflets to addressing the

---

[77] *PWB Combat Team...*, 48.
[78] Konrad Kellen, *Katzenellenbogen*, 111.
[79] *PWB Combat Team...*, 61.
[80] *PWB Combat Team...*, 62-63.

enemy directly by loudspeaker at the front. Whereas the authors of leaflets to be shot in artillery shells were constrained spatially by the size of the paper on which their appeals could be printed, those making direct loudspeaker appeals were constrained by time; it was dangerous to speak for more than 90 seconds when one was vulnerable to gunfire and artillery shells at the front. The soldiers at Sharpe practiced making these addresses, as well.

Finally, Habe held a course in contemporary history:

> We boned up on the names of politicians and military men that were mentioned in the news, we memorized what parties they belonged to, which organizations they represented, and the abbreviations by which these organizations were known. We had to be able to name immediately the participants in important conferences, and also, of course, the results of these conferences. We learned which newspapers represented whose interests, who financed them, which important men wrote for them.[81]

Stefan Heym recalled that "Habe was not the only instructor in Camp Sharpe, but the others, who lectured mostly on technical matters [the technicalities of broadcasting and printing] remained shadows."[82]

Occasionally, the soldiers at Sharpe slipped up. The Czech actor Walter Kohner (4th MRB company) recalled that there were:

> Trucks with loudspeakers and transmitters [...] parked behind our barracks. We were testing the equipment, broadcasting within the confines of the camp. Once, one of the company's chief technicians accidentally transmitted on a frequency outside his range. The citizens of Gettysburg were mystified to hear orders over their radios "to surrender to the Americans" delivered in German.[83]

While Habe's students were learning all the ins and outs of propa-

---

[81] Hanuš Bruger, *Der Frühling war es wert*, 142.
[82] Stefan Heym, *Nachruf*, 265.
[83] Hanna and Walter Kohner, *Hanna and Walter: A Love Story*, 133. Walter Kohner emigrated to the United States in 1938, one year after completing his studies at the Max Reinhardt Seminar in Vienna.

ganda, the other divisions, too, were active in their own fields. Under the instruction of their company officers, the radio personnel tested and ordered their equipment. Lieutenant Arthur Jaffe recalls:

> The four 400-watt mobile transmitters were tested in code broadcasts from one to the other, the longest distance covered being the 20 miles between Camp Ritchie and Camp Sharpe. Since no tuning equipment was available, the transmitters could not be adjusted for operations in the broadcast band but this was later accomplished in the Theater of Operations.[84]

Once an antenna tower had been erected at the camp, and the FCC had granted a frequency, the 1 kilowatt station played music for a day, that could be picked up in the town of Gettysburg.

Because the first group of printers at Camp Sharpe didn't have any equipment, they were sent to a lithographic school in New York City for specialized training in vari-type printing.

The men in the motor pool not only had to learn how to drive and maintain the widest variety of army vehicles at the camp, but to prepare these vehicles for the invasion of France. In selecting the men who would be driving the propagandists around Europe, preference was given to those who not only possessed advanced driving skills, but who also had exceptional linguistic skills. Eddie E. Amicone, for example, had worked for Railway Express in Youngstown, Ohio, prior to his enrollment in the army, but he also happened to have been born in Argentina to Italian parents. He says, of his training at Camp Sharpe: "We learned how to drive all kinds of army vehicles there. And we had to waterproof the motors on the vehicles to take them from the landing crafts to land." In any off time that they had, the drivers had to prepare for fighting: "We had to learn how to fire all sorts of army weapons, including a M-1 and Springfield. We learned how to use hand grenades. Then we went through physical training on an obstacle course (crawling under barbed wire and over walls)."[85]

While all the men were given some military training and prepared for firing weaponry, not all of them were particularly adept in these areas. Walter Kohner recalled one of their more comic "war games":

---

[84] [Arthur Jaffe], *History, Second Mobile Radio Broadcasting Company*, 19.
[85] Letter to the author from Eddie Amicone, 22 Nov. 2013.

On one field exercise we roamed for forty-eight hours through the fields and forests of Pennsylvania and Maryland to play "invasion." The German front was so carefully duplicated that some of the soldiers dressed in German uniforms not only were captured by our own units and interrogated, but also by some Gettysburg farmers, who took them for escaped POWs.[86]

It is not surprising that the farmers made this error, since Walter Kohner belonged to the 4th MRB, and, by the time he was stationed at Camp Sharpe, there was a German prisoner of war camp also located on the battlefield.

Iowan native Clyde Shives, of the 5th MRB, recalled that the company "was shown dozens of training films, [and] went on hikes [...]. Basic training was placed under the supervision of Lt. Robert Asti, a Field Artillery lieutenant, who made the hours under the broiling Pennsylvania sun interesting if not enjoyable at times."[87]

All the Sharpe men, of course, had to become familiar with army weaponry. They "learned how to throw grenades, fire the bazooka, launch rifle-grenades and wallow through the infiltration course." Lieutenant Arthur Jaffe reported that "The high point of this training was the day the company traveled to Ritchie to fire the M-1 on the snowbound rifle range. Although the weather was freezing and a blizzard obscured the targets, over 90 percent of the men qualified."[88]

Even so, many of the propaganda specialists had difficulty with this portion of their training. Si Lewen, of the 3rd MRB company, was a slight man of 5 feet 2 ½ inches; he had particular difficulty handling "the 'clumsy' M1 rifle, unable to even hit the target or learn to 'squeeze' the trigger." He would get rid of his heavy rifle as soon as he got to France, and substitute a lighter carbine for it.[89] Albert Guerard, of the 2nd MRB showed a similar lack of prowess with rifles:

> Stefan Heym [...] told my wife I would hardly survive, since I was unable to handle my gun. The kindly Leon Edel [...] reassured her. And I did pass the rifle range test that was mandatory prior to shipping overseas. Firing into the snow, I even had an astonishingly good score. My scorer, once the re-

---

[86] Hanna and Walter Kohner, *Hanna and Walter: A Love Story*, 133.
[87] [Clyde Shives], "History of the Fifth," *5th Mobile Broadcasting Company*.
[88] [Arthur Jaffe], *History, Second Mobile Radio Broadcasting Company*, 20.
[89] Author correspondence with Si Lewen, 23 Jan. 2014.

sults had been officially recorded, told me I had, in fact, been hitting the wrong target.[90]

A sign, perhaps, that the men of Camp Sharpe had radically different interests from the men in most infantry units is the fact that when, in February 1944, Albert Guerard's college novel *The Hunted* got a positive review in *The New York Times*, his executive officer, Lieutenant Arthur Jaffe, posted the review on the company bulletin board for all to see.

There was not a lot of spare time at Camp Sharpe, but in their class breaks and in their down time, the men often talked politics. Many of the men, especially those who had been born and raised in Germany, were concerned about how the Allied nations would deal with a defeated Germany after the war. Their discussions could sometimes become rather heated as they debated the various possibilities and the advantages and disadvantages of each—be it a matter of re-education programs or mass punishments, Allied occupation or German independence.

For quite another reason, Stefan Heym, as an enlisted man, sensed occasional tension between himself and a couple of the commissioned officers at the camp. Heym had a healthy ego, and ascribed this tension to these officers' own sense of inadequacy:

> It is only among the officers that there are no experts of any kind; one speaks Italian, another some German, nothing more. That creates a strange, not very healthy relationship between the officers, or at least some of them, and the men in training. The officers have evidently been ordered to go easy on the gentlemen artists; on the other hand their feeling of inferiority towards these men causes a resentment towards them of which they are perhaps not even aware.[91]

As one of these officers, Lieutenant Hans Habe, too, found the going sometimes difficult, remarking, some years later, that "To shape this 'unit of geniuses' [...] into military companies was not an entirely enviable task. I confess that now and again I handled those 'geniuses' pretty roughly, both during training and later at the Front." He would

---

[90] Albert J. Guerard, *The Touch of Time*, 64.
[91] Stefan Heym, *Nachruf*, 262-263.

point out, however, that he was not any easier on himself: "At Camp Sharp[e] I worked twelve or more hours a day."[92]

Because of the secrecy of the camp's mission, only the commissioned officers were allowed to go to the bars in downtown Gettysburg; noncommissioned officers were not allowed to drink there.[93] But for nearly all the men, "when evening came the men headed for Gettysburg [...] for relaxation and peace from the doggedness of army life."[94] It was a twenty-minute walk into town, and the men chose a variety of entertainments there, based on their personal interests. When the Rangers-in-training had gone into town, they did not have any Class-A uniforms to wear, but only their fatigues. Gunter Kosse recalls that this created a little sensation in town, since the girls there had never seen men in fatigues before. They always asked about their "mission" and regarded them as heroes. There was not a lot of socializing, though; mostly the men went to the movie theaters or to the soda fountain.[95]

There wasn't a lot of socializing between the MRB men and the other townspeople, either. Ed Alexander remembers spending time in the town library and going quite often to the movies[96]; Philip Pines remembers the drugstore and soda fountain on the first floor of the David Wills House.[97] The men visited the town's various eating establishments: Mitchell's on the Square, Lincoln Logs out on York Street, Ned's Place and Mrs. Smith's Restaurant on Chambersburg Street.[98] Mrs. Smith's Restaurant was famous for its chicken dinners and its home-baked pies, and one could get an excellent meal there for one dollar.[99]

Some, but not all, took advantage of their location by touring the Gettysburg Battlefield, both with and without official guides. Some of the men could even claim ancestors who had fought there: Lieutenant

---

[92] Hans Habe, *All My Sins*, 342.
[93] Interview with Si Lewen, 26 July 2013.
[94] [Clyde Shives], "History of the Fifth," *5th Mobile Radio Broadcasting Company*.
[95] Author interview with Gunter Kosse, 23 Sept. 2013.
[96] Author interview with Edward Alexander, 21 June 2013.
[97] Author interview with Philip Pines, 15 Aug. 2013.
[98] [Clyde E. Shives], "History of the Fifth," *5th Mobile Radio Broadcasting Company*.
[99] Interview with Philip Pines, 15 Aug. 2013.

Gordon Frick, 2nd MRB company, had an ancestor in the Union army, Colonel Jacob Frick, who had led the 27th Pennsylvania Emergency Militia during the Gettysburg campaign. Lieutenant Frick organized his own tour for men interested in learning more about the battle. Lieutenant Gaston Lewis Pender, 4th MRB company, could claim blood ties with William Dorsey Pender, who was the youngest major general in the Confederate army, had led a division of Confederate soldiers at Gettysburg, and died of a wound he received there.

There were occasional special dinners and socials organized solely for the men at Sharpe. The beer flowed freely on these occasions, and the men frequently put on entertainment in the form of songs and skits. Milton R. Stern, of the 4th MRB company, remembered the preparations they made for their farewell banquet-beer party:

> The beer was easy enough. So [the cook] Steinberg and I looked around. Steinberg has a feeling for flowers, so we've got to collect flowers. Where do you collect flowers? Off soldiers' graves, naturally. So we go out and we visit a lady, who is in a nice house near Union graves. We said, "Can we pick these flowers because we are going to have this—?" "Oh, sure, sure." So we picked all the flowers we needed from off the soldiers' graves. It was really quite something. Then we had our beer party [...] in the VFW headquarters post in town.[100]

Arthur Jaffe of the 2nd MRB company recalled that "One of the highlights of [our] stay at Sharpe was a Washington's Birthday dance at the Gettysburg Armory, at which members of the company presented several original skits."[101]

The later MRB companies could not use the Armory for their banquets, because a group of fifty German war prisoners were brought in and housed there. This made for odd exchanges whenever the men from Sharpe passed by it on their walks into town. Ed Alexander, of the 5th MRB company, remembers the Armory and the fence that surrounded it:

> I distinctly recall a metal fence upon which the German soldiers leaned and joked with us freely with no U.S. guards in

---

[100] Interview with Milton R. Stern, conducted in 1992 by Ann Lage.
[101] [Arthur H. Jaffe], *History, Second Mobile Radio Broadcasting Company*, 20.

sight. They teased us about secrecy, adding that American soldiers who all spoke German surely had some other purpose in their training at "your special camp." Whenever they mentioned the camp, it was accompanied by a knowing smile. I cannot say whether any of our guys ever spilled the beans, but these POWs had either been captured or surrendered because of leaflets we were being trained to prepare—how ironical! In any case, we could never pass them on our way into Gettysburg without their hailing us in German. But I cannot believe they ever knew exactly what we were about. My guess is that, because we all knew German, they suspected we were in U.S. Intelligence. If so, they were not far from the truth.[102]

The main gathering place in Gettysburg was the Gettysburg Hotel on the town's center square. Here families and girlfriends came to stay, because they sensed that the Camp Sharpe men would soon be going abroad. Igor Cassini's brother Oleg and Oleg's wife, actress Gene Tierney, came to visit while Igor was stationed there. Igor's mother, the Countess Marguerite Cassini, moved to Gettysburg for the entire period her son was at Sharpe. After the hotel became too expensive for her, she took a room in Miss Gilliland's boarding house on Carlisle Street, but:

> The countess spent all her days in the Hotel lobby, using the Hotel stationery and having her mail delivered there. She had a small [white] bulldog named "Cigarette" and often startled guests as she walked through the lobby calling "Cigarette! Cigarette!" with her heavy accent. One gentleman apologized that he had no cigarettes, and she became highly insulted![103]

Eventually, the Countess was evicted even from her boarding house when Miss Gilliland discovered that the Countess, strict war rationing to the contrary, had stolen two steaks for herself and her son.[104]

While some wives and girlfriends took semi-permanent residence

---

[102] Correspondence from Edward Alexander, 28 June 2013.
[103] Elise Scharf Fox, *Hotel Gettysburg, A Landmark In Our Nation's History*, 79.
[104] Elise Scharf Fox, *Hotel Gettysburg, A Landmark In Our Nation's History*, 158.

at the Hotel, many could not afford it and took rooms in town. Fred Perutz's wife Margaret, for example, found a room close to the camp and commuted daily to a clerical job in Hagerstown, Maryland. Sylvia Ziffer, whose husband Ewald was with Perutz in the 4th MRB company, also took a room in town; she organized a "Service Wives Club" in Gettysburg for the wives of the Sharpe soldiers. They met socially at the USO headquarters located in the Hill House on Chambersburg Street; they also met weekly at the Red Cross headquarters in the Topper Building on Baltimore Street, where they wrapped and rolled bandages for the war.[105]

Of course not all the soldiers were fortunate enough to have their wives and girlfriends so close at hand. Otto Schoeppler (2nd MRB company) spent most evenings in the barracks, writing letters to Eva Marie Saint, his girlfriend at Bowling Green State University.[106] Others waited eagerly for the much-coveted 2- or 3-day passes, when they could hitchhike to their homes or to a larger city. Every Saturday afternoon, a bus pulled up outside Camp Sharpe to carry men to the Harrisburg train station, so that they could catch a train for all points east.[107]

Because the men at Sharpe were all pledged to extreme secrecy regarding their classes and their mission, it was difficult for any deeper relationships to form between the single soldiers and the women in Gettysburg. However, two soldiers did indeed marry local girls during their assignments there. Both were commissioned officers. The first was Lieutenant Clarence ("Ace") Seemann, of the 3rd MRB Company, a North Dakota native most recently residing in Aberdeen, South Dakota; he married Bertha Josephine ("Jo") Howe, a teacher of commercial subjects at Gettysburg High School. The ceremony took place on April 23, 1944, at St. Paul's Evangelical Lutheran church in Biglerville. The couple was attended by Kathryn Dentler, a neighbor of the bride and a sixth-grade teacher at the Lincoln School in Gettysburg, and by Lieutenant Gaston Lewis Pender, a North Carolina native assigned to the 4th MRB company. Shortly after the wedding Seemann was shipped

---

[105] See "'Service Wives' Club Is Planned," *Gettysburg Times*, 19 Apr. 1944, and "Seven Service Wives in Club," *Gettysburg Star and Sentinal*, 6 May 1944.

[106] Schoeppler was born in a small Rhenish village in Germany, but had emigrated to the U.S. with his parents in 1928. Eva Marie Saint would later make her name as a screen and stage actress.

[107] [Clyde Shives] "History of the Fifth," *5th Mobile Radio Broadcasting Company*.

off for further training in England, and he was therefore unable to attend the July 1st wedding of his friend Gaston Pender to Kathryn Dentler in the same Biglerville church. Pender's commanding officer, Captain Joseph Goularte, filled in as best man, while Miss Dentler's sister served this time as maid of honor. Just before the wedding ceremony, Major John T. Jarecki pinned the silver bar of First Lieutenant on Gaston Pender's uniform. The camp cook sent some men out to polish up all the bronze plaques near the camp and illuminate the name of William Dorsey Pender, so that "when [Pender] came by with his bride, he could see it."[108] Several days later, Pender was shipped to Europe.

He was one of the last to depart. A month earlier, news had reached the States of the Allied invasion of Normandy, France. Walter Kohner and Robert Breuer (both of the 4th MRB company) were in New York on a three-day furlough when the call came for all military personnel on leave to return to their units immediately and prepare for departure to England. Both the 2nd and 3rd MRB companies had already left. In their last days in Gettysburg, these men had "[fought] for passes, even if only for a single evening,"[109] Stefan Heym recalled:

> These long but oh so short evenings! People sit together in the dining room of the hotel, married couples and couples who don't yet have the official blessing, the men not acting very military in spite of their uniforms, the women in the fashion of the day, padded shoulders, waist-length jackets, hems reaching just under the knee; one strives for a little festivity, the waiter has put candles on the table, the little flames flicker now and again, and when one of the women laughs, all too often it sounds forced. [...A]fter dessert they go to the room, take a bath, and sleep together until the phone jangles; at four o'clock in the morning the hotel porter awakens the gentleman soldiers.[110]

The wives and sweethearts learned about the departure date even before the soldiers did. No one at the camp had broken the oath of secrecy regarding departure; the local tailor had simply mentioned to one of the soldier's wives that he had to "iron the uniforms of the of-

---

[108] Interview with Milton R. Stern, conducted in 1992 by Ann Lage.
[109] Stefan Heym, *Nachruf*, 263.
[110] Stefan Heym, *Nachruf*, 263.

ficers, because it's all starting up tomorrow."[111] In the flurry of activity that followed, quite a number of soldiers, like Stefan Heym, managed to get married.

The first signs of departure at the Camp had been "two massive gleaming army trucks, one at each barracks of the 2nd and 3rd Mobile Broadcasting Companies. These were broadcasting and printing trucks especially constructed for us."[112] It was, Leon Edel marveled, "a corporation executive's dream—an assembly of transmitters, microphones, and printing presses, ingeniously laid out within the narrow confines of the deluxe vehicles. The trucks, with their sleek chrome and plastic interiors, seemed like pieces of Hollywood science fiction, though of course we didn't dare say that."[113] The 2nd and 3rd MRBs would cross the channel with these trucks and with the water-proofed vehicles of the motor pool, right after the invasion of Normandy.

The 4th and 5th companies had an even more hurried departure from Gettysburg. Hans Habe was called up early: "The training of the four units was not yet completed when I was transferred to London."[114] Lieutenant Arthur Hadley[115] was ordered to join the 5th MRB company at Camp Sharpe just five days before it was ordered to depart for France. He was not impressed with his new company: "Confusion is endemic to the Fifth MRB, its men and officers. [...] Many have not even been through basic training or fired their rifles or pistols." Some of the men had been "foisted off" on the Fifth MRB "from units wishing to get rid of their foul-ups and oddballs. Orders are usual[ly] obeyed in the Fifth MRB, but only after international negotiations."[116] On Hadley's second day in Gettysburg, the unit captain asked for volunteers to help two inexperienced Norwegian riggers take down the Camp's 80-foot antenna tower and pack it up for shipment to France. Hadley volunteered, as did two of the company's propaganda team:

> By the end of the day we managed to get down three or four sections. It becomes obvious the tower will not be ready

---

[111] Hanuš Burger, *Der Frühling war es wert*, 145.
[112] Leon Edel, *The Visitable Past*, 24.
[113] Leon Edel, *The Visitable Past*, 25.
[114] Hans Habe, *All My Sins*, 342.
[115] Arthur Hadley, born in New York, enlisted in the army directly out of high school.
[116] Arthur T. Hadley, *Heads or Tails*, 85.

to go to Europe. Not even half ready. The bottom of the tower pivots on a huge single bolt. Perhaps we can swing the whole tower down side wise on that bolt. None of us knows, but we have no real choice. [...] With care we line up trucks, winches, and attach wires to parts of the tower. The massed truck engines roar. The tower swings forward. The tower hesitates. The tower collapses in a crumbled broken mass resembling a heap of gigantic bent and severed hairpins. [...] The captain gathers a task force to cover the debacle with paperwork. If Adolph [sic] Hitler had spies watching the Fifth Mobile Radio Broadcasting Company, he would have had reason to hope for victory.[117]

On July 15, 1944, a Gettysburg newspaper remarked that, "It's unfortunate that Gettysburg is to lose Camp George H. Sharpe. The camp will move to another site on August 1, to be replaced by a labor camp." It remarked that the town would miss the men of the MRBs: "Camp Sharpe was not a large camp and there was little or no publicity attending its operation here. But to have several hundred men moving in and out of town every few months and the occasional Army vehicle passing through the streets gave this historic little community a little touch of the war-spirit."[118]

After the last of the soldiers had moved out of Gettysburg, the Camp Sharpe buildings were used to house German prisoners of war. It was becoming evident, even to the town of Gettysburg, that the European war had entered its final phase.

---

[117] Arthur T. Hadley, *Heads or Tails*, 85-86.
[118] "Here and There," *The Star and Sentinel*, 15 July 1944.

Chapter 3

Preparations in Britain

The eight-day crossing on D Deck of the Mauretania, like slow death in the Lincoln Tunnel, was worse than any battle I later had to cover.

Louis de Milhau, one of my pals in the 5th, recalls that when we were first ushered down to the bowels of the ship—all portholes closed for security reasons—my reaction was pure café society.

"Don't worry," I said. "We won't stay here. It's just a place to put our stuff, like checking your coat in a club."

Not so. We stayed. The food was murder. It came around in large garbage pails, oatmeal and hard-boiled eggs, both in the same pail.[119]

Most of the Sharpe soldiers, like the majority of American enlisted men, made the crossing to Europe on cruise ships that had been refitted to hold the largest possible number of bodies. The men of the 2nd and 3rd MRBs crossed on the *Queen Elizabeth*. Many of the 4th and 5th MRB men went on somewhat smaller liners. It was an unpleasant journey for everyone, but Igor Cassini, with his aristocratic sensibilities, was particularly incensed. "It was drummed into us by the army itself that we were a special baby and would have special care. So where did they put us on board ship? If you could call it a ship?"[120]

Actually, Cassini's crossing was probably better than some; he was at least on a Cunard cruise ship. Some of the MRB men, like Arthur Hadley of the 5th MRB, made the crossing on an "ancient, remodeled tramp freighter."[121] A select few, like Lieutenant Hans Habe and Albert Rosenberg's special team of interrogators, went by plane.

The *Queen Elizabeth* had been converted soon after its launching into a troopship capable of carrying 5,000 troops from Australia to the

---

[119] Igor Cassini, *I'd do it all over again*, 95.
[120] Igor Cassini, *I'd do it all over again*, 95.
[121] Arthur T. Hadley, *Heads or Tails*, 86.

Suez Canal. After the United States entered the war, however, the *Queen*'s route was changed to the North Atlantic, and its capacity was increased to 15,000 men per crossing.[122] This capacity allowed for an entire military division to cross the ocean at one time, but, as Stefan Heym pointed out, it was "not a division, but rather a conglomeration of troops of all branches of the armed services, along with all sorts of reinforcement units, staffs, and special units like the 2nd Mobile Radio Broadcasting Company, all with their luggage; in addition, weapons, war materials, munitions: a single torpedo, more or less in the engine room, God help us."[123]

Eddie Amicone, of the 2nd MRB, remembers that 1000 of the 15,000 passengers aboard the *Queen Elizabeth* were service women. As for the food that was served there, it "was terrible! It was greasy English food." Furthermore, "the soldiers weren't allowed to smoke on the deck of the ship because the spark from the cigarette could be seen from German submarines."[124]

It was especially difficult for the men to sleep decently:

> There are too many men on board. There is not enough space below deck for everyone to sleep there, especially since each officer must have his own bed in a cabin; so the troops sleep by turns for half the night below deck, in every accessible space, in hallways and on stairs, and can't sleep, because down there it is too narrow and too hot and the air is too stuffy, while their comrades up on deck, lying on hard planks, cannot sleep either in the raw, moist wind, which makes one shiver in spite of a wool blanket and coat, and because somebody is always stumbling over them.[125]

Hanuš Burger, Heym's Czech friend, described the daily ritual:

> We could sleep for eight hours; then we were allowed for four hours to stand around or walk, because there was no room to sit. A meal followed, in the enormous dining room, then another four hours of standing, and after the second meal

---

[122] This change in route and in troop numbers supplied by Henrik Ljungström, *Queen Elizabeth, 1940-1973*.
[123] Stefan Heym, *Nachruf*, 269.
[124] Letter to author from Eddie Amicone, 22 Nov. 2013.
[125] Stefan Heym, *Nachruf*, 270.

the same thing. Finally we had to shake awake the momentary occupant of our hammock and, for eight hours, it was ours again.[126]

There was, however, occasional entertainment. Private Joe Louis, boxer and Heavyweight Champion of the World, put on demonstration matches on shipboard. The men from Camp Sharpe also took some initiatives in relieving the tedium of the crossing. Stefan Heym and Albert Guerard produced a daily newspaper called the *Ocean News*. Using the talents they had acquired in their news monitoring classes at Camp Sharpe, the two men gathered their material by listening to the news programs of the BBC and the American radio stations in the ship's radio room. They had an added benefit in return: they were allowed to sleep in the radio room instead of in the crowded quarters below deck.

Meanwhile, Hanuš Burger got involved in producing a variety show for the soldiers, using the professional and amateur talent available among the men on board. The show was scheduled for the day before the ship's arrival in Glasgow, and the troupe had to perform it six times, in order to accommodate the numbers and sleeping schedules of everyone:

> At the end of the show we all came out on stage, white, brown and black soldiers, hooked arms and sang a song to a Shostakovich tune composed by Lance Corporal [Peter] Weidenreich.[127] The text said that we were determined to create a new world after our triumph over fascism, in which nationality and the color of one's skin would no longer be an issue. Every time we were applauded frenetically, and afterwards we went to the dining hall, where they wanted to separate us—whites from coloreds—as was customary. We protested and organized a hunger strike.

The admiral stepped in as mediator, the army officers remanded the order, and the dining hall was integrated. Burger exulted: "My God, were we proud..."[128]

---

[126] Hanuš Burger, *Der Frühling war es wert*, 147.
[127] I.e. Peter Wyden.
[128] Hanuš Burger, *Der Frühling war es wert*, 149. The European-Jewish Sharpe Boys were all sensitive to discrimination in all forms, having experienced it
continued...

Another event that alleviated the men's boredom—and perhaps alarmed them—during the crossing was a mock submarine attack, "with the *Queen Elizabeth* sending out the finned instrument that appeared about to destroy her."[129]

The ships of the Cunard line were fast ships, generally requiring four and a half to five days to cross the Atlantic; during the war years, however, the crossings could take up to eight days. That was because they never followed a direct course from New York to Britain; they took an unpredictable route to avoid any confrontations with submarines that might otherwise be lying in wait for them. Philip Pines remembers, "At one point, the weather got very warm, and it was rumored that we were near the Canary Islands, but I can't say for sure that that was the case."[130] Because the ships were not protected from hostile submarines by a slower-moving convoy, they relied both on speed and maneuverability to avoid hostile confrontations.

It was not particularly comforting to the men to have the ship constantly shift course. Pines remembers how, on the last night aboard the *Queen Elizabeth*, the ship was "no longer changing course every six minutes, but now every minute, and the ship veered from side to side, making it extremely difficult for a man to remain in his bunk."[131]

On April 5th, the *Queen Elizabeth* docked in Glasgow; as the Sharpe Boys disembarked with their rifles and duffle bags, they were greeted by a kilted Dutchman at the dock, given doughnuts and coffee, then loaded on a train for a day-long trip to Wotton-under-Edge, a small village nestled in the southern edge of the Cotswold mountains. Philip Pines had a miserable journey; although he had not been at all seasick on the crossing, he now became violently "land sick," and was still so miserable and dizzy upon his arrival, that his fellows had to help him into his bunk at Wotton-under-Edge. The 2nd and 3rd MRB men were housed here in 30 tents erected on a hillside that looked

---

...continued
    themselves in Europe. Hans Habe happened to land in France with a Black battalion; he commented that "The few weeks which I spent with the coloured soldiers induced me to write *Walk in Darkness*, which was published in 1948" (Habe, *All My Sins*, 343). This novel tells the story of an American Black GI in occupied Germany.

[129] Albert J. Guerard, *The Touch of Time,* 64.
[130] Author interview with Philip Pines, 15 Aug. 2013.
[131] Author interview with Philip Pines, 15 Aug. 2013.

down on the town. During their stay, the townspeople came to ask them to join them in a game of soccer. Fortunately, the Europeans in the unit knew the game and were happy to oblige.

Here, in Wotton-under-Edge:

> The propaganda section discussed the history of Europe and the political situations and personalities responsible for the war; the radio technicians studied operational circuit diagrams to refresh their minds and to get further practice; the wireless technicians practiced code-sending with a couple of keys they were able to rig up with local materials; the printers discussed printing techniques; the drivers tuned up their vehicles for the hard combat driving that lay ahead.[132]

In mid-April, the men were moved to Clevedon, in Somersetshire, where the 2nd MRB "was attached to the First U.S. Army through the 72nd Publicity Service Battalion."[133] Clevedon was a small coastal town that had reached its heyday during the Victorian era, when it had been developed into a picturesque summer resort. It was, the English now said with understated disdain, "a nice place, where people go to die."[134] Here the men got more training from British officers.

The crossings—and arrivals—for the 4th and 5th MRBs were not much different from those for the 2nd and 3rd, except that the ships were a bit smaller and held only 5,000 to 7,000 soldiers. Many of the 4th MRB sailed on the Cunard liner *Mauretania*; most of the 5th on the U.S.S. *Uruguay*.[135] As on the *Queen Elizabeth*, some of the men on the *Uruguay* provided distraction for the long sea voyage. The radio crew kept busy repairing the ship's sound system, while Corporal John P. Barricelli provided piano entertainment on the promenade deck. Members of the propaganda section edited and announced daily newscasts over the sound system, while Technical Sergeant Leopold Ruff, a

---

[132] [Arthur H. Jaffe] *History, Second Mobile Radio Broadcasting Company*, 23.
[133] [Arthur H. Jaffe] *History, Second Mobile Radio Broadcasting Company*, 23. This was the first training center set up for P & PW units. Other centers were set up in cooperation with other bodies such as PSD/SHAEF, OWI, and OSS at London Brondesbury, Watford, Caversham, and Burton-on-the-Hill. See Ray K. Craft, *Psychological Warfare in the European Theater of Operation*, 14.
[134] Author interview with Philip Pines, 15 Aug. 2013.
[135] The "Uruguay," built in 1928, was originally named "California."

Belgian-American, gave French lessons.[136] When they arrived in Britain, they, like their predecessors, received further training in British intelligence.

Unlike their MRB brothers from Gettysburg, Private Gunter Kosse and the other commandos trained at Camp Sharpe had been sent, not to England, but to Donaghadee, in Northern Ireland, for their further training. Here they enjoyed the unusually warm, sunny weather, and interacted with the locals, both through soccer games and visits to Irish homes. One unusual interaction occurred when, as part of their training, some of the men had to put on German uniforms, and neighboring locals got frightened and called out the home guard.[137]

From Donaghadee the men were shipped to Manchester, to replacement depots, to be assigned to various units. After a visit from a major from General Eisenhower's SHAEF headquarters, it was decided that training these men for high-risk activity behind German lines was simply not cost effective, since the Nazis had captured previous teams before they could provide intelligence and/or engage in sabotage. All activities in Manchester were frozen, and the men suddenly had nothing to do except to practice their interrogation techniques on the prisoners of war who had been brought to Manchester as farm workers. Kosse found the situation rather ironic. Of the 80-100 men who had been sent to Manchester for assignment and training, a number spoke fluent Italian. Nevertheless, the soldiers were confined to camp at night, while the Italian war prisoners walked around freely.

Since the men stationed in Manchester couldn't engage in interrogation practice all the time, they helped out with work at the depots; Kosse remembers stenciling the symbols of rank onto officers' steel helmets. He speculates that the freezing of all activity in Manchester probably saved his life. Instead of crossing the Channel for D-Day, the men in his company had to wait until September for their new war assignments. Kosse was assigned to IPW (Interrogation of Prisoners of War) Team 4, and attached to the 8th Infantry Divisiion, XV Corps. This team was made up of six men, all of whom came from different parts of Germany and Austria. The idea was that their varied geographies would make it possible to communicate more intimately with the widest possible range of German prisoners.

---

[136] [Clyde Shives], "History of the Fifth," *5ᵗʰ Mobile Radio Broadcasting Company*.

[137] Author interview with Gunter Kosse, 23 Sept. 2013.

Philip Pines remembers clearly his stay in Clevedon, where the broadcasting men from the 2nd MRB were sent for training. There they found four two-and-a-half-ton trucks with transmitters to work with; Pines was assigned to a unit with two trailer trucks. His truck had a big broadcasting Preston1 KW wireless transmitter. The second truck had a radio studio on its truck bed, called a "doghouse," from which broadcasts were made and sent to his transmitter truck. Three BBC engineers supervised the men's training; they also "conducted a thorough screening of the officers and enlisted men designated as radio technicians and made certain that all were qualified to handle the equipment."[138] The 2nd MRB men were then sent to Tyntesfield, a camp 20 miles south of Bristol. There the radiomen received the American equipment that had been shipped from Camp Sharpe, and more. Tyntesfield was a tiny camp, but there was a PX unit there, and a camouflage engineer battalion with camouflaged trucks. This battalion had the task of setting up seemingly regular units of fake tanks and landing craft, in order to make the Axis armies believe, incorrectly, that the Allies were gathering for action some place other than the beaches of Normandy.

Meanwhile, the propagandists were sent to Watford near London to partake in a series of tests to determine their future assignments. For ten days the men were subjected to aptitude tests, tests of courage, obstacle courses, psychological examinations, and so on. They were then sent on to Brondesbury Park, in the East End of London, to study at the Psychological Warfare School of the British army. Brondesbury was an area that came under heavy bombing; here the men learned, after a few embarrassing overreactions to the sound of incoming buzz bombs, "to behave like the English, who slept in subway shelters but otherwise went about business and pleasure as usual."[139] The men were housed in middle class villas, enjoyed warm baths and high tea, and were, in general, treated as gentlemen rather than as lowly soldiers.[140] In their off time, the men were able to enjoy the amenities of London, where many of them seemed eager to live up to the American GIs' reputation as being "overpaid, overfed, and oversexed."[141]

For two weeks the men in propaganda "heard lectures and partici-

---

[138] [Arthur H. Jaffe] *History, Second Mobile Radio Broadcasting Company*, 23.
[139] Igor Cassini, *I'd do it all over again*, 96.
[140] Stefan Heym, *Nachruf*, 277.
[141] Igo Cassini, *I'd do it all over again*, 96.

pated in discussions on propaganda work in the field, new directives on the writing of leaflets and the preparation of loudspeaker appeals and on the overall plan for the 'psychological attack' on the Germans."[142] All the men found the instruction given them by the British military officers to be extremely beneficial. At Camp Sharpe, Hans Habe had assumed the role of six or seven men in order to prepare and deliver lectures on all aspects of wartime propaganda. In taking on this herculean task, he had been hampered by the fact that he was a pioneer in this area of intelligence training in the United States. Britain had a long history of international espionage and intelligence work and had already been putting this knowledge into use since the 1939 outbreak of the war. Otto Schoeppler remembers Habe's lectures as being "more strategic than tactical."[143] In England, however, the men felt that every moment of instruction was relevant to the immediate task at hand:

> Here the course material is different, more demanding than at Camp Sharpe, more academic. Here one gives intelligence tests that really demand intelligence; here psychology is taught, psychology of the masses and the individual, problems are treated, people as prisoners [...], and the instructors carry themselves as if they were wearing, indiscernibly, the academic robes of Oxford dons.[144]

At Brondesbury Park the men from Camp Sharpe studied the finer psychological categories that existed among the German soldiers and civilians they would encounter. They worked with the material that the British Lieutenant Colonel Henry V. Dicks[145] had created, called "Psychological Foundations of the Wehrmacht," which distinguished five distinct categories of response to Nazism among young German soldiers. These five were: fanatical "hard-core" Nazis; modified Nazis "with reservations"; "unpolitical" Germans; passive anti-Nazis; and active anti-Nazis. These categories could be further distinguished; the so-called "hard-core" Nazis, for example, would include not only "party toughs," but also "idealistic zealots," and "concealed fanatics," while the "unpoliticals" would encompass rural populations, village artisans,

---

[142] [Arthur H. Jaffe] *History, Second Mobile Radio Broadcasting Company*, 25.
[143] Letter to author from Otto Schoeppler, 18 Aug. 2013.
[144] Stefan Heym, *Nachruf*, 277.
[145] Dicks was a specialist in psychological medicine and, in civilian life, Professor of Psychiatry at the University of Leeds.

minor officials, and professional soldiers.[146]

In addition, the interrogators learned that, in order to be truly helpful to those in military intelligence who analyzed and quantified information taken from deserters and prisoners, their questions must be similar or nearly identical.[147] To this end, Lt. Colonel Dicks had, with the collaboration of American sociologist Edward Shils, devised a questionnaire that the interrogators should follow. This included, in addition to the prisoners' attitudes regarding National Socialism, Hitler, the other Nazi leaders, conditions at the home front, their immediate officers, and rivalries in the Wehrmacht, their attitudes regarding the outcome of the war, their specific concerns about Allied occupation, and their post-war expectations, as well as their current feeling of political responsibility and war guilt.[148]

At Brondesbury Park, then, the men learned the tactical techniques that would prove especially valuable in the field. Si Lewen echoed the feelings of many in his company when he said that he received a great deal more practical training in England than he had at Camp Sharpe. From Brondesbury, he was sent to Southampton for several weeks, and he was trained there for loudspeaker work. He was also trained for "white flag missions," something that Hans Habe had never covered in his instruction. White flag missions were those where opposing sides would meet and negotiate. Lewen now learned how he, as an interpreter on such missions, could help further America's cause through "creative translation," that is, by adjusting the language of the English-speaking generals according to his own knowledge of how Germans respond to certain words and phrases.[149]

After their two-week stint at the British Intelligence school, Bert Anger[150] and Otto Schoeppler were approached "in a very clandestine manner" with an offer to join the OSS.[151] The OSS [Office of Strategic Services] was the creation of William J. "Wild Bill" Donovan, and was

---

[146] See Daniel Lerner, *Psychological Warfare against Nazi Germany*, 135-143.
[147] Daniel Lerner, *Psychological Warfare against Nazi Germany*, 109.
[148] See Daniel Lerner, 121-124, for the standard interrogation form devised by Dicks and Shils.
[149] Author interview with Si Lewen, 26 July, 2013.
[150] Bert Anger was a native of Düsseldorf, Germany. Because of his father's political affiliations, the family was forced to leave Germany when Bert was sixteen. He was a graduate of Dartmouth College at the time of his entrance into the war.
[151] Letter from Otto Schoeppler to author, 18 Aug. 2013.

involved not only with intelligence, but with espionage on the European front—and with much of the "black" propaganda that was practiced by the Americans. "Right from the beginning," Si Lewen recalls, "there was some cooperation [between the OSS and the MRBs], both on the tactical as well as strategic level." He remembers that the OSS held a "special interest, even fascination" for the men in military intelligence. Although the OSS had begun primarily as a civilian organization, during the course of the war there was more and more mixing of civilians and enlisted men in the various undertakings of the civilian propaganda agencies. The basic difference between the two organizations, Lewen has noted, was that "the OSS was primarily a spy agency, whereas [the] MRB Companies' mission was Psychological Warfare."[152] Many of the MRB men would eventually transfer into the OSS, but, at this early stage of preparations for the Normandy landings, although Bert Anger and Otto Schoeppler were "eager to accept, [...] someone in the chain of command refused to release us."[153]

The later MRB companies would remember their training at Brondesbury Park as much for the rigors and physicality of the training as for the contents of their lectures. Clyde Shives[154] noted that the men "were given physical endurance tests, the like of which we had never seen in the States. The physical training strongly indicated preparation for combat." He noted, however, that "the men [also] received technical training along the lines of information control in an occupation area," an indication, certainly, of the Allied leaders' "confidence of an early victory."[155]

Once this basic training was over, the MRB men gathered at Tyntesfield to wait for the coming invasion. The radio and wireless men, mechanics and drivers had further training there. The propaganda unit of the 2nd MRB commuted daily to Clevedon for more work in the preparation of radio material, leaflet writing, and the interrogation of prisoners of war. They were also interviewed a second time by representatives of Colonel Clifford R. Powell; Powell had been put in

---

[152] Letter from Si Lewen to author, 28 Aug. 2013.
[153] Letter from Otto Schoeppler to author, 18 Aug. 2013.
[154] Clyde Shives was born in Iowa, but went to California at age nineteen and never returned. He trained in plumbing and foundry work before enlisting in the U.S. Army.
[155] [Clyde Shives] "History of the Fifth," *5th Mobile Radio Broadcasting Company*.

charge of Psychological Warfare Division activities for the 12th Army Group[156] and was "planning the overall tactical psychological warfare activities for the imminent invasion."[157] Some men were sent to London to study the preparation of leaflets for dissemination by artillery shell, and carried out experiments in firing the shells under varying conditions. Their training finally over, the men had little to do except participate in occasional military drills. During this period, Stefan Heym finished a war novel that he had begun working on in the States, entitled *Of Smiling Peace*.

While the bulk of MRB men were waiting for their post D-Day assignments, several "early lift" groups began leaving the camp in small teams. Hanuš Burger volunteered to be part of a three-person team that would be among the earliest of MRB units to make the crossing to Normandy, a team that included a Polish-born graduate of Camp Sharpe named Samson Knoll.[158] One member of the team would write the first French newspapers for a newly liberated France, one would compose tactical pamphlets, and one would address the German soldiers by loudspeaker from the front lines, and try to get them to surrender. Burger volunteered for the loudspeaker position.[159]

The military intelligence teams that were now formed were not made up solely of American GIs; Englishmen were mixed in with the American teams. Hanuš Burger's team was placed under the command of George Langelaan, a British intelligence officer who had been born in France.[160] The only teams that had already been established in Gettysburg were pairings of soldiers for interrogation purposes. Otto Schoeppler and Bert Anger had been paired by their commanding officer at Camp Sharpe; this and other pairings were based on obvious

---

[156] The 12th Army Group was under the command of General Omar Bradley; it was made up of the U.S. 1st Army, commanded by General Courtney Hodges; the U.S. 3rd Army, commanded by General George Patton; and the U.S. 9th Army, commanded by General William H. Simpson. See Frank Prosser and SGM Herbert A. Friedman (Ret.) "Organization of the United States Propaganda Effort During World War II."

[157] [Arthur H. Jaffe] *History, Second Mobile Radio Broadcasting Company*, 25.

[158] Although born in Poland, Knoll had moved to Berlin at age two, and had studied history and German literature at Berlin's Humboldt University, until forced to flee to Paris in 1933. From there he went to London, and in 1935 he emigrated to the United States, where he worked as a teacher prior to his enlistment.

[159] Hanuš Burger, *Der Frühling war es wert*, 156.

[160] Hanuš Burger, *Der Frühling war es wert*, 159.

compatibility between the men involved.¹⁶¹ In the field, however, the men were shifted around among the troops as needed. "There would be a dozen teams of, say, a driver, interrogator, and photographer. But maybe if they needed a photographer and didn't have one on hand, they could get one from another company. So everybody knew everybody pretty well."¹⁶²

Furthermore, some companies, like the 5th MRB, already merged in Britain with the 4th MRB, which had arrived previously. As Arthur Hadley relates it:

> The merged units then divide up into teams that will be attached to various Army headquarters to do their assigned work. As the war progresses and more of Europe gets liberated, some will go to Eisenhower's Supreme Headquarters in Versailles to write leaflets, some will go to Paris or Luxembourg to run major radio stations, others to various prisoner-of-war cages to provide intelligence on German morale.¹⁶³

In this manner, "the teams were parceled out to various psychological warfare units in Europe. Some of them were assigned to psychological warfare at SHAEF Supreme Headquarters, Allied Expeditionary Force, 12th Army Group, and each of the U.S. field armies had a psychological warfare detachment."¹⁶⁴

The radio men were the first to be called for embarkation to Normandy. Lieutenant Gordon Frick and members of the wireless section were "assigned to communications duties aboard the First Army Command Ship." They "moved across the Channel on D-Day and remained on duty off the Normandy Coast all through the early stages of the fighting."¹⁶⁵

Hanuš Burger was unusual in having his propaganda team already sent to France on the evening of the D-Day invasion. Lieutenant Jacob Tennenbaum landed on Omaha Beach on D-Day plus 2 on an advance intelligence-gathering expedition. Most of the men in the 2nd and 3rd MRB units were sent a few days later, when the fighting was less in-

---

¹⁶¹ Interview with Arthur Jaffe, 15 July 2013.
¹⁶² Interview with Arthur Jaffe, 15 July 2013.
¹⁶³ Arthur T. Hadley, *Heads or Tales*, 86.
¹⁶⁴ Interview with Max W. Kraus by Cliff Groce, 1988.
¹⁶⁵ [Arthur H. Jaffe] *History, Second Mobile Radio Broadcasting Company*, 31.

tense. These teams departed on various days, with various ships. Stefan Heym, Oskar Seidlin, Peter Wyden, and the two technicians who accompanied them crossed on D-day plus 6, Si Lewen's team on D-day plus 9, Albert J. Guerard's, on D-day plus 10, Radio Technician Philip Pines's team made its crossing on D-day plus 26 because of a twelve day delay in repairing a loading dock destroyed in a storm. Eddie Amicone was one of the Camp Sharpe drivers who made the crossing with the waterproofed vehicles that carried loudspeakers, printing, and broadcasting equipment to mainland France. The plan was that they should cross in small teams, and then meet up as a complete company in late June.

Stefan Heym had several explanations for why the 2nd and 3rd MRB companies were split into small teams of only four or five men for the Normandy landings:

> Ostensibly [they did it] because the higher officers wanted to avoid the complete loss of so many splendid, specially trained heads and, more importantly, of the printing equipment and transmission apparatuses, that could not be replaced very quickly. Or, more simply, [they sent them in later] because the guns of the ships and tanks were firing at that time, and the gentle barking of the loudspeakers would have died away piteously.[166]

The MRB men had all been trained in their special branches of psychological warfare, but some were still adjusting to the idea of unquestioned obedience at the front. This showed up already at the crossing. Hanuš Burger, for example, refused to wear the military underwear given to all the men before the crossing because it stank of an agent designed to protect the wearer from gas attack.[167] Oskar Seidlin[168] froze and refused the order to climb down the rope nets from the transport vessel to the landing craft, even though this maneuver, called "landing under fire" had been practiced before the men's departure

---

[166] Stefan Heym, *Nachruf*, 284.
[167] Hanuš Burger, *Der Frühling war es wert*, 156-157.
[168] Oskar Seidlin was born Oskar Koplowitz, to a Jewish family in what is now southwestern Poland. He emigrated to Switzerland in 1933, and received a doctorate from the University of Basle three years later. He came to the United States in 1938 and was teaching at Smith College when called up to military service.

from the States. Eventually he had to be picked up and thrown across from one ship to the other.[169] As another soldier from the 3rd MRB put it: "Climbing down the nets in the dark was very scary"; because of this and the many frightening adventures that lay ahead of him, he doubtless spoke for many of the Camp Sharpe men when he added, "I went in the service as a boy and came out a man."[170]

Si Lewen seconded the fear that came over the men upon their initial contact with orders to put themselves in danger:

> Just before landing on "Omaha Beach," the convoy came under enemy air attack and everybody was ordered below deck. I was well trained and obedient, but common sense told me that had the ship been hit, everyone below deck would certainly have drowned. In the darkened bowels of the ship, which only increased the sound and concussions of the nearby exploding bombs, I trembled and my heart pounded so hard and loud I thought my chest would burst; I felt faint and began praying. I loathed myself, not only for being a coward, but a hypocrite as well—after the "all clear" sounded.[171]

Even the later channel crossings of the 4th and 5th MRB companies were not without danger. Ed Alexander recalls that the Channel was teeming with German submarines when he made his crossing in early fall. The men on his ship were ordered to stay below deck, since a total blackout was being maintained throughout the crossing. Many of the men came down with a violent case of food poisoning, however, and disobeyed orders by running into the open air above deck. Fortunately, the ship made it to the Normandy coast, although the ship directly behind it was torpedoed.[172]

As part of the first team of MRB men to land at Omaha Beach on the morning of June 7th, Samson Knoll was immediately assigned the task of interrogating captured Germans on the beach before they were sent to prison camps in England. Hanuš Burger, on the other hand, was sent alone inland to one of the first, temporary, prisoner "cages" that had been set up near Trévières. He arrived after dark, but found

---

[169] Stefan Heym, *Nachruf*, 286.
[170] Douglas G. Fish. Cited in Tom Brokaw, *An Album of Memories*, 90.
[171] Si Lewen, *Reflections and Repercussions*, Chapter 18.
[172] Author interview with Edward Alexander, 21 June 2013.

the shelling too fierce for him to do anything but seek shelter near the prisoners[173].

In Isigny-sur-Mer, a town of fewer than 3,000 people, the reunited Knoll-Burger team was finally able to make the first broadcast to a freed French city from a truck with mounted loudspeakers. Burger was especially touched when, as ordered, he played the national anthems of France, the U.S., Britain, and Russia, and saw French children, women, and old men emerge from the ruins of what had appeared to be a completely abandoned town. The townspeople were all still in shock from the heavy bombardments, all with tears in their eyes at the realization that they were now in Allied hands.[174]

The MRB men continued to filter into France in the days and weeks that followed. Those of the 2nd and 3rd MRB companies entered in June through August, those of the 4th and 5th from September through November. In Europe the MRB broadcasting units, like the MRB propaganda units, were divided into groups:

> The big broadcasting systems guys disappeared, I didn't know where to. Eventually, they became General Bradley's transmitting station to the United States, with a big 15 KW transmitter; I saw this later, at Verdun.
> I remained with the two trailer trucks [one with a big broadcasting transmitter; one with a studio "doghouse"] and we landed in Normandy for the first broadcasts to England and, from there, to the States. Our call letters were JESQ, or, in radio language, "Jig Easy Sugar Queen." I stayed with the trucks for the rest of the war.[175]

Philip Pines remembers that, when they landed in France with their broadcasting equipment, mines were still being cleared away from the beaches.

The MRB men were soon active overall, broadcasting, interrogating, writing propaganda leaflets. Stefan Heym received what he considered a somewhat crazy assignment: he was ordered to write a propaganda piece that would be dropped into the German lines on July 4th.

---

[173] Hanuš Burger, *Der Frühling war es wert*, 166.
[174] Hanuš Burger, *Der Frühling war es wert*, 167-168.
[175] Author interview with Philip Pines, 15 Aug. 2013.

This speech, Heym was told, should inform the enemy soldiers of the importance of this American holiday. The maneuver was impressively staged:

> There are fireworks, forty-eight rounds fired from forty-eight artillery guns, and then the leaflet comes from the clouds explaining the sudden cannonade, in words that reveal the deep feelings Sergeant S. H. has for a revolutionary, democratic America: "On July 4th 1776 the United States was born as a nation—a nation of free people, equal before the law and willing to govern themselves. We went to war in 1776 to defend these freedoms. And we are fighting for these freedoms today. No tyrant should venture to force his will on a people, on Europe, or on the world." Upon which he appealed directly to the recipients of the leaflet, "And what are you fighting for?"[176]

After landing in Normandy, Si Lewen, too, was assigned the task of persuading the German soldiers to surrender, both by leaflet and by loudspeaker. The existential fear that he had himself experienced upon entering the war zone inspired him to make a suggestion for leaflets that would appeal more directly to the German soldiers:

> Soon after landing in Normandy, I realized that offering only the traditional choice of "death or surrender" was useless against soldiers trained to follow orders—obediently. "Don't mention politics, or allude to their 'loved ones at home'; even patriotism becomes lost on a battlefield. Just convey definite, simple instructions on 'how to surrender,'" I proposed to my superiors, and then devised a simple phonetic way to teach enemy soldiers a few simple steps: "Ei ssorenda" would become the basic message of every leaflet and every loudspeaker appeal directed into enemy lines, together with a few simple steps on "how to surrender." Repeated over and over, this tactic proved increasingly effective. Eventually, I learned from some just captured prisoners, that long before surrendering, they had practiced among themselves the "correct" pronunciation. "Ei ssorenda" became an insidious challenge, intruding into enemy minds and eventually the trigger for surrender. Subtly and

---

[176] Stefan Heym, *Nachruf*, 292-293.

obliquely, the strategy—call it brainwashing—worked.[177]

There were two reasons for the success of repeating, in pamphlet and loudspeaker form, the correct pronunciation of "I surrender" in the Allied appeals. First, it "made the German familiar and at home with the idea of surrender, so that the switch-over to action became that much easier."[178] And secondly, on a more practical level, it gave the German soldiers confidence that they could make their wishes known at once to the Allied soldiers and, by doing so, lessen the risk of their being shot in error.

The Camp Sharpe men were showing, immediately upon their landing in Normandy, that they had been well trained for a difficult task. Whether serving as drivers, interrogators, radiomen, or "hog callers," these "psycho boys" were fighting effectively, and they were doing it in order to save, not take, the lives of Allied and German soldiers.

---

[177] Si Lewen, *Reflections and Repercussions: A Memoir*, Chapter 18. Art Jaffe reported that, during the Brittany campaign, about twenty different leaflets were prepared, all written by Si Lewen, and more than a million copies printed for distribution, so that "everyone had heard of [these leaflets] after the first couple of weeks of operation." Arthur Jaffe, *History, Second Mobile Radio Broadcasting Company*, 51.

[178] *History: P & PW*, p. 149. Cited in David Lerner, *Psychological Warfare against Nazi Germany*, 216-217.

Chapter 4

The Struggle for France

> *I remember how my ears suddenly acquired a new dimension—I heard the sounds of our engines, the cracking of branches and twigs, a bird song, a few whispers among our guides. We were soldiers who had not yet had the experience of fearing that guns might open up at any time, and I told myself that a thousand variants of such situations—more dangerous and terrifying—could be told by other soldiers and guerrillas. During the unclocked minutes of our stealthy progress, I learned how blinding fright can take hold while the mind remains active and vigilant. I clutched my weapon. My ears and eyes somehow became centers of the self. And my mouth had a singular dryness.*[179]

The men from Camp Sharpe had been forced to make a sudden and immediate adjustment to wartime conditions when they landed at Normandy. Here they had their first experiences in a war zone; here they saw their first dead bodies. Here they experienced, for the first time, the putrid stench of death.

In spite of this, they began at once to perform those duties for which they had been trained: interrogating prisoners, setting up radio capabilities, monitoring news, writing and printing propaganda pamphlets, chauffeuring officers to the front lines, speaking directly to the troops by microphone. They had been split into teams in England. Now they were dispersed among the different army units in France and had to learn how to conquer their fear in order to function efficiently. Si Lewen was immediately sent out to address the Germans by loudspeaker, as a "hog caller." He recalls:

> Often, on the way to an assignment, I was afraid, and fearful that my voice would betray me. But during the very first encounter with the enemy, the voice I heard did not sound what I had feared would be my voice. The army training had done its job—transformed whatever I had been into a soldier,

---

[179] Leon Edel, *The Visitable Past*, 64.

almost mechanically, automatically doing what a soldier was meant to do. I was no longer the man I was, or thought I was. When the tactical situation was right—mostly when the Germans were surrounded—the demand to surrender was successful. Occasionally it was met with a salvo, or worse. Afterwards, at night, I would drink myself into a stupor.[180]

One MRB team (made up of intelligence men, one leaflet writer, one recording expert, one artillery liaison officer, one general liaison officer and four men to operate a 250-watt British loudspeaker unit) came under the leadership of the intelligence officer Lieutenant Jacob Tennenbaum. The resources of this team were immediately put to the test when the VII Corps at Utah Beach asked for assistance in bringing about the surrender of some surrounded German troops, and the corps' Deputy Chief of Staff for Intelligence (G-2) asked for a new, tactical pamphlet to be shot across the German lines. The "prestige of Psychological Warfare was at stake in this its first test in combat operations," Arthur Jaffe remembers. Because the men did not yet have their printing equipment, "a mimeographed leaflet was therefore hurriedly prepared in German to meet the emergency."[181] For further printing, the team took over a local printing shop in Bayeux, where the French printers were put to work helping set the type for further leaflets. After the next request came, the printers managed to produce 38,000 leaflets on a hand press; their MRB teammates rolled and loaded them into shells, and a crew travelled to the front to deliver them to the artillery batteries. "It was later reported that within a couple of hours 30 German soldiers deserted to our lines with the leaflets in their hands," Jaffe reported proudly. "Thus, on 16 June, Psychological Warfare had its first notable combat success in the west front fighting."[182] Three days later, nine more company men joined this initial team.

It became standard practice for the Sharpe soldiers, whether by leaflet or by loudspeaker, to speak to the Germans as one fellow soldier speaking to another. Si Lewen, for example, might open his appeal by speaking about that morning's breakfast—"shit on a shingle," explaining to the Germans that this was actually "a rather tasty creamed beef on toast."[183] The MRB men had been instructed never to speak ill

---

[180] Si Lewen, *Reflections and Repercussions*, Ch. 18.
[181] Arthur H. Jaffe, *History, 2nd Mobile Radio Broadcasting Company*, 32.
[182] Arthur H. Jaffe, *History, 2nd Mobile Radio Broadcasting Company*, 32.
[183] Si Lewen, *Reflections and Repercussions*, Ch. 18.

of Russia, but Lewen broke this interdiction by describing the latest advance of the Russian army in the East and then asking directly: "Who do you want to reach Berlin first, the Americans or the Russians?"[184] This was followed by a call to "end this 'damn war.' It's time you get home, make babies, rebuild Germany."[185]

Hans Deppisch was one of the most effective "hog callers" in the European campaign, doubtless because of the personal history that he brought to his efforts as one of the oldest members of the 2nd MRB company. During the First World War he had commanded forces on the German side, before being captured by the Americans in 1918. In the intervening years he had moved to America, studied economics and languages, married, and started a family. He was 44 when he enlisted in the U.S. army in 1943. The fact that Deppisch had been a German soldier, been captured and treated decently as a POW in the last war, undoubtedly lent credibility to his appeals.[186]

Meanwhile, many of the MRB men sent to interrogate prisoners in the POW "cages" set up in northern France were surprised to find unusual groupings among them: "The men who speak the same language have found each other. There are Poles and Walloons, Georgians and Turkomen, Czechs and Alsatians, French and Italians—and Germans." It soon became clear that the Germans had begun "to highjack men of all nations into the German Army, forcing them first into the labor battalion and later right into the front lines."[187] It was fortunate that so many of the men who'd trained at Sharpe were fluent in languages other than French and German; Edward Alexander, for example, had originally been selected for the MRB companies because of his fluency in Armenian. The "hog callers" were already addressing the enemy forces in Polish as well as German. This mix of nationalities created a greater difficulty for the Allied command: "Are Poles, who shot their German officers and came to our lines to be treated as ordinary prisoners? And what about the poor muzhik from Astrakhan, who was captured by the Germans at Bialystok in 1941, was starved and beaten until he became a defender of the New Order in a German 'Ost-Battalion'?" Many of these men were invaluable to the interrogation

---

[184] Author interview with Si Lewen, 26 July 2013.
[185] Si Lewen, *Reflections and Repercussions*, Ch. 18.
[186] Deppisch was awarded both the Bronze Star and the Croix de Guerre for his service. He, Bert Anger, and Otto Schoeppler were the only non-commissioned officers of the 2nd MRB company to receive both awards.
[187] Stefan Heym, "I Am Only a Little Man," 9.

teams, since they were more willing than most Germans to provide information regarding morale in the German army. From them the Allies quickly learned that the linguistic situation in the German army had become so bad that there were "units in which the commanding officer needed an interpreter to get his orders across."[188]

While the men whose responsibility was appealing to the Germans by leaflet and by loudspeaker spoke to the Germans as fellow soldiers who shared the same fears and longings as they did, the MRB interrogators soon discovered that most of the German soldiers were, in fact, quite different from the American and British troops, in that they had been brainwashed to adhere strictly to the Party line and never to question anything they saw going on around them. Hanuš Burger, for example, described a typical interview with a captured sergeant in which he inquired about his peacetime activities:

> "You're a teacher?"
> "Senior secondary-school instructor." He was insulted, because I had said "teacher."
> "Your discipline?"
> "German, History, Geography."
> "Dangerous subjects, aren't they?"
> "How so?"
> "Well, German, for example. Did you read [...the Jewish poet] Heine with your students?
> "Yes, we did him. In as much as he is close to the people."
> "What, for example?"
> "The folk songs, the Lorelei..."
> "With an indication that he was the author?"
> "Of course not."
> "Of course?"
> "What do you want...? After all, I am only a little teacher."[189]

Samson Knoll discovered, right away, that every one of the German prisoners he interrogated protested, when asked about his political views: "I am just a little man. I don't understand anything about

---

[188] Stefan Heym, "I Am Only a Little Man," 9.
[189] Hanuš Burger, *1212 sendet*, 45. All translations from this work are my own.

politics."[190]

Most of Knoll's investigations confirmed his worst suspicions of the degree of the Germans' anti-Semitism. One soldier, who insisted that "if I had been responsible for these crimes, I could not live with myself," then told Knoll that he had seen how a secret military police squad had massacred a group of sixty Jews—old men, women and children. He had not inquired about it, because "there must have been a reason for it. [...] They must have done something." Knoll pressed the soldier, pointing out that small children could hardly have done something deserving of a death sentence. He then asked the soldier if *he* would have fired on the Jews if he had been part of the police squad. The soldier squirmed, saying, "Orders are orders," and maintaining that the police probably also felt uncomfortable about killing the Jews. When Knoll then asked him what the difference was between killing Jews and slaughtering pigs, the soldier answered, "There is a huge difference. [...] When I slaughter a pig, I think of all the good things I can eat, ham and bacon and all that." Knoll concluded: "That is for me the decisive element in Nazism in particular, and in fascism and racism in general. 'Jew' and 'human being' did not go together for him... That was the education at Ordensburg![191] That was twelve years of service in the [Nazi] party! That is the beginning of the Holocaust!—of every Holocaust!"[192]

Knoll found a single exception to Party brainwashing among those he interrogated in France—a German staff sergeant whom he questioned just outside Cherbourg. This soldier had been a student of German literature in Munich, and he was selected as "representative" of a certain class of German soldier and subjected to a "prolonged interrogation."[193] Knoll questioned him for five hours. "And he knew instinctively what I wanted from him. That is, what I wanted to learn from him. And he did not want to indulge me. I also knew instinctively that he knew what I wanted. And I didn't want to indulge him, ei-

---

[190] Bernsdorff, Walter and Martin Vialon, "Vom Um-Erzieher zum Freund," 37. All translations from this interview are my own.

[191] Ordensburg—"Order," or "School Castles," were built as the places where the future leadership of the Third Reich should be trained. Three such castles were built, but the program was never fully implemented.

[192] Bernsdorff, Walter and Martin Vialon, "Vom Um-Erzieher zum Freund," 39-40.

[193] See Daniel Lerner, *Psychological Warfare against Nazi Germany*, 109-117, for a discussion of the methods of Psychological Warfare Interrogation.

ther." Again and again Knoll pressed him:

> "You are a student of literature. Let's look at folk songs; here we have the Lorelei, for example, one can't imagine the German folk song without the Lorelei, and here it says on the score 'Author unknown,' doesn't it? And yet you know that it is by Heine, one of the greatest poets of the German language! And then, how about Mendelssohn [...]." He didn't admit anything, and I went on and on and on in this manner.

Finally, the soldier broke, saying he couldn't go on any more, he was "in prison shock." Knoll released the man, and then, later in the morning when he emerged from his tent, he saw the prisoner again:

> I went up to him and asked: "Does the world look better now the sun is shining?" He smiled, and then he said: "You know, I knew exactly what you wanted to hear from me. But I will not do anything, I will not say anything, that could get me treated differently from the way my comrades are being treated. When the war is over, you will find me on the side that I assume you want to find me on. But not now."

Knoll added: "That is the only German soldier whose hand I shook. I often think of him and am very curious about what happened to him."[194]

Like Samson Knoll, Stefan Heym found that most of the captured Germans were "drained of moral courage" after over a decade of Nazi brainwashing.[195] But he, too, found a couple of exceptions among the prisoners he questioned:

> There was a soldier from Saxony, a textile worker, who approached the interrogator strolling through the cage, buttonholed him and said, "You don't mind if I tell you something?"
> "No."
> "I want to say... And then he blurted out, "What a shame it is for the Wehrmacht that a German has to go to a prison

---

[194] Bernsdorff, Walter and Martin Vialon, "Vom Um-Erzieher zum Freund," 37-38.
[195] Stefan Heym, "I Am Only a Little Man," 44.

camp to breathe feely again and feel like a man!"

There was a young paratrooper from the Rhineland, 22 years of age, who confided after a lengthy interrogation that he had been a secret courier for Pastor Martin Niemoeller's Confessional Church.

Still, Heym noted that, in spite of these exceptions, "this better element in Germany" had "neither a common program nor a common organization strong enough to be effective" in leading a true resistance movement.[196]

After the Allies had secured the beaches of Normandy, the main body of the 2nd MRB was sent to Colombières, to join the Twelfth United States Army Group operating from the Colombières chateau. Here they met up with the advance team of radiomen who had already set up their mobile SCR 399 transmitter in Colombières and were broadcasting reports about the frontline fighting to England.[197] The war correspondents had already left to join the Press Camp, but OWI and OSS civilians remained behind.

Arthur Jaffe recalls that German bombers flew over Colombières twelve times during their first night there. One of his youngest soldiers "went crazy" and had to be taken away to a hospital. When Jaffe visited the next morning, he found him confined in a strait jacket. Jaffe considered the young soldier the first "casualty" of his unit. He was not killed by enemy fire, but he had been destroyed by the noise of the bombers.[198]

Quarters in the Colombières chateau were reserved for civilians, officers, journalists and "by two future members of De Gaulle's cabinet," while the enlisted men were forced to sleep in foxholes outside the moat. Albert Guerard recalls:

> We shaved from a greenish watery scum drawn from the moat in helmets and slept under an airplane's jettisoned gasoline tank split open to provide cover. [...] Now and then we raided a great tureen of water kept simmering in the kitchen, for the use of officers and civilians only, and at least twice (trembling violently as I sat) I used the castle's only known sit-down and forbidden toilet, entered through a small door in the

---

[196] Stefan Heym, "I Am Only a Little Man," 45.
[197] Arthur H. Jaffe, *History, 2nd Mobile Radio Broadcasting Company*, 31.
[198] Author interview with Arthur Jaffe, 29 Dec. 2013.

outside wall.[199]

Guerard adds that his MRB included professors and writers, who were "ruined by years of soft living. [...] So unobtrusively we found our way, secretly and one by one, to a rude unfinished attic, where we could sleep on the broad crossbeams."[200] The officers eventually learned of this, but left well enough alone.

Colombières provided the company with its first prolonged stay under combat conditions; the front lines were "only three miles forward and the beaches just four miles to the rear."[201] The men dug foxholes or slit trenches and dove into them for shelter during the nightly air raids. They had to worry not only about the bombings, but about shell fragments from their own anti-aircraft batteries, and it became quite common for the soldiers to keep their helmets on even while sleeping:

> There were rumors that the Germans would attack with gas. One guy from the propaganda unit on the road, Boris Kremenliev [a musicologist from the 2nd MRB], suddenly heard the alarm "gas." He fired three shots and yelled, "Gas, gas!" All the guys grabbed their gas masks and put them on; those who were without them jumped into the moat. Later, Lieutenant Salvatori said to Kremenliev that he had almost killed his own men with his warning shots, and asked what he would do if the alarm came again? Kremenliev answered that he would do the same thing all over again.[202]

During the day the men were kept busy interrogating local civilians and prisoners of war; Albert Guerard was sent to Cherbourg to interview some restive Arabs who had just been released from German forced labor camps only to be conscripted into French army labor battalions.[203] Meanwhile, a monitoring section under propaganda officer Lieutenant Arthur Vogel covered all the radio broadcasts made by German and Allied radio stations and news services. These formed the basis for the radio broadcasts, loudspeaker appeals, and tactical leaflets.

---

[199] Albert Guerard, *The Touch of Time*, 73.
[200] Albert Guerard, *The Touch of Time*, 73.
[201] Arthur H. Jaffe, *History, 2nd Mobile Radio Broadcasting Company*, 33.
[202] Author interview with Philip Pines, 15 Aug. 2013.
[203] Albert Guerard, *The Touch of Time*, 73.

From late June to the end of July, the 2nd MRB printing section turned out over 2 million copies of about fifteen different leaflets.[204] A reporter who visited the mobile unit during this time wrote, with some amazement,

> Authors, psychologists, newspaper men and college professors [prepare] scripts and messages. They confer in shot-up houses and in tents, and when they are not conferring they are absorbed in reading heavy literature. Among them are Germans, Czechs, Poles, Hungarians, French and serious-looking Englishmen.
> With them are large vans which have been converted into printing offices, radio stations and photographic dark rooms. Pamphlets are being printed which, encased in shells, are hurled against the Germans. There are also passenger cars with loud speakers on their roofs, patrolling nearby villages and spreading the gospel of good will. In one town not far back of the lines a printing press has been salvaged which turns out a paper that is showered down on unretrieved, nearby France.[205]

On one occasion, during a lull in his broadcasting assignments, Philip Pines was sent to an ammunition supply point ASP 128, probably the first supply point for the 28th Division in Normandy. He was there to replace the smoke canisters in the artillery shells with rolls of propaganda leaflets.[206] He stayed there for five or six days, sleeping in a field where the 105 millimeter artillery ammunition was stored. There were the bodies of dead Germans in the field next to where he slept. He recalls how the humidity at night caused the odor of death to spread across the fields and permeate everything, including his clothing and his hair. In addition to the nighttime stench, Pines was fearful of the German bombers that came over every night, since he was sleeping so close to the ammunition supply. When he discovered that the men who loaded the shells were sleeping where it was somewhat more pro-

---

[204] Arthur H. Jaffe, *History, 2nd Mobile Radio Broadcasting Company*, 34.
[205] S. J. Woolf, "Battle of Bulletins Frays Enemy Nerves," *Geneva Daily Times* 11 July 1944.
[206] Generally, 105 mm shells were used. Each shell held 500 leaflets. The larger 155 mm Howitzer smoke shell held about 1,500 leaflets, but the smaller shells were cheaper and more efficient. Ray K. Craft, *Psychological Warfare in the European Theater of Operation*, 38.

tected, he went over there at night to sleep in a slit trench.[207]

In spite of the company's overall effectiveness in broadcast and leaflet propaganda services, it was still regarded with some skepticism and even scorn by the regular army. Arthur Jaffe noted that:

> With the team's enlarged staff, it was possible to devote more time to a problem which had not been seen in its true light in training—the correction of misapprehensions on the part of staff officers as to the functions and capacities of psychological warfare. To this end, liaison with staff sections was given close attention, and from then on it was considered one of the key factors in the conduct of successful operations.[208]

In his memoirs, Hanuš Burger recalls overhearing his commander, Captain Maxwell Grabove, being threatened by a major from the 12th Army group. This major told the captain that his MRB men were enjoying the safety of the Chateau Colombières, but that they had not, as yet, persuaded a single German soldier to surrender. If this did not change immediately, the major said, the captain and all his men would be reassigned to infantry.[209] The next morning Hanuš Burger was sent, with a driver and technician, to make an appeal in the St. Lo sector, where the Americans were attempting to break through the enemy lines and establish a route to Paris. Here the fighting was especially fierce. As Burger tells it, the three men rode in a Jeep out beyond the front lines, where they came immediately under German fire. An even greater danger seemed imminent when low-flying American war planes appeared on the horizon: "For an instant I wondered whether a Kraut in his foxhole looks significantly different from a GI, when one is observing him from above."[210] As soon as the planes had passed overhead, Burger made his appeal to the Germans: "Attention, attention, you Krauts! Come out of those holes [...]. Surrender, otherwise my captain will have to go to the front."[211] Within the next few minutes, seventeen paratroopers and one armored infantryman had surrendered to him. Three of the men were already severely wounded: one seventeen-year-

---

[207] Author interview with Philip Pines, 15 Aug. 2013.
[208] Arthur H. Jaffe, *History, 2nd Mobile Radio Broadcasting Company*, 33.
[209] Hanuš Burger, *Der Frühling war es wert*, 173-174.
[210] Hanuš Burger, *Der Frühling war es wert*, 179.
[211] Hanuš Burger, *Der Frühling war es wert*, 179.

old had been blinded by an explosion close to his eyes; one had had his left arm shot off above the elbow, and one corporal had been hit twice in the stomach. Burger managed to fight his inclination to feel pity for the three only by recalling the Germans' treatment of his Czech friends: "You are 17. And Jirka, whom they hanged in Prague, he, too, was 17."[212] In spite of the poor condition of the young Germans, the Americans were jubilant: "Eighteen Krauts, who will no longer shoot at them! The technician and I naturally know quite well, that it was not our laughable loudspeakers that achieved this success, but rather the low-flying aircraft. Or the eighteen men had enough of it all anyway."[213]

Still, this MRB action was enough to change the attitude of the infantrymen who'd witnessed it. Captain Jaffe reported the reaction of one of them:

> When he saw the crew go out in front of the forward lines and set up the speaker less than 50 yards from the enemy, with small arms fire all the while peppering their vehicle, and then saw the number of prisoners that responded to the appeal by surrendering, he commented: "I guess I was wrong. Why the hell don't you guys bring that thing up here all the time?"[214]

Burger commented, "I realize now that there [was] one real hero among us. The driver, [John] Billy, who quietly sat at the steering wheel and didn't budge, to be able to drive away when necessary. He winks at me when I walk off with the eighteen supermen that stumble along with us."[215]

As the war progressed, the loudspeaker appeals began to follow a particular pattern:

> This work was new to us and the Army, and we made up our rules as we went along. Through interviews with prisoners, we soon discovered that reminding Germans that they would be treated according to the Geneva Conventions was one of the most effective ways to persuade them to surrender.

---

[212] H. H. Burger, "Episode on the Western Front," 52.
[213] Hanuš Burger, *Der Frühling war es wert*, 180.
[214] Arthur H. Jaffe, *History, 2ⁿᵈ Mobile Radio Broadcasting Company*, 35.
[215] H. H. Burger, "Episode on the Western Front," 52.

Our broadcasts, then, took on the following structure: first, we'd outline what we knew about the German position; second, we'd describe the weight of artillery and air power that was about to fall on them; finally, we'd end with assurances that those troops who surrendered would be well treated under the Geneva Conventions.[216]

As a member of IPW Team 4, Gunter Kosse had a most unusual confrontation later on in the war that proved that the Germans knew the terms of the Geneva Convention quite well:

Three doctors came over under a white flag to complain that the Americans were firing on their hospital. This was not true, the one doctor simply wanted to desert. I said that I would have to send them all back, since they had come under the white flag; we had to follow the Geneva Convention. The doctor took out a Leica camera then and began taking pictures. This was against the Geneva Convention. And the doctor said, "So, you must arrest me as a spy." We did. And I discovered, afterwards, that the man had no film in his camera![217]

On July 7th Captain Maxwell Grabove was able to report to headquarters that during the month of June, the 2nd MRB company had fired approximately 1000 rounds, containing 700,000 leaflets, across enemy lines, and that, of the approximately 2000 Germans who had surrendered to the Allies, 70 percent had read the leaflets, and approximately 20 percent "surrendered with leaflets on their person."[218] He reported, too, that although the company concentrated on the German enemy, it did not neglect the French civilian population. The public address units serving the civilian communities were "received with an overwhelming enthusiasm by civilians, civil and military authorities. Their arrival in a community is often awaited by a gathering from 200 to 1000 people."[219] Furthermore, the company had begun on June 14th to publish a one-sheet newspaper in Isigny. It was called *The Liberator*; it was published daily and distributed over a number of lo-

---

[216] Arthur T. Hadley, "Firing Potent Words, From a Tank," *New York Times*, 25 Sept. 2006.
[217] Author interview with Gunter Kosse, 9 Oct. 2013.
[218] Maxwell Grabove, report of 7 July, 1944. In AG 319.1, Vol. 1
[219] Maxwell Grabove, report of 7 July, 1944. In AG 319.1, Vol. 1.

calities in liberated France. Technical sergeant Leon Adolphe Dreyfus (2nd MRB) edited this paper. Dreyfus must have felt the irony in being the editor of liberated France's first newspaper, since he was a descendant of the French captain Alfred Dreyfus, who had been falsely accused—and convicted—of having communicated French military secrets to the Germans some fifty years before the Normandy invasion.[220]

In spite of all these successes, the MRB men still had difficulty convincing some infantry of the benefits of the leaflets and loudspeaker appeals. To many it seemed a waste to load shells with leaflets rather than ammunition. To help alleviate this problem, the MRB men printed leaflets in English as well as German, so that the infantrymen could read the materials that they were firing into enemy lines. They also began firing these leaflets only at dawn or at dusk, once it was learned that the German soldiers were reluctant to pick up any leaflets by daylight, when their commanders could see them.

As for the loudspeaker appeals, they were dangerous for the MRB men who made them; they were dangerous for the Germans who chose surrender and risked being shot by their own men; and they were dangerous for the troops, since the appeals frequently drew intense shelling in their direction. Nor could anyone absolutely guarantee that one particular loudspeaker appeal would result in the surrender of any Germans. In August, for example, the American newspapers carried a story by Tom Wolf, who accompanied several of the 2nd MRB men—Lieutenant Irving B. Mickey (commanding officer), Sergeant Fred Messinger (German announcer), Corporal Stephen Lisiecki (Polish announcer and technician), and Private Talmadge Huey Powhatan (driver and technician)—on one of their "hog calls." Wolf watched them string their wires and set up their microphone 300 yards from the Germans, and listened as they told the Germans how, "in about 15 minutes we will shell your positions with smoke to give you an opportunity to come to our lines unobserved. Your highest duty is to save your lives for your families and for a new Germany. Decide now." Wolf reported that, "No prisoners came in that night. A couple were heard to call 'Kamerad'[221] when Messinger got through speaking.

---

[220] In 1946 Leon Dreyfus would petition the courts to change his name to Leon Andrew Dale.

[221] The Germans indicated their willingness to surrender by calling out that they were ready to become "comrades" with the American soldiers.

But they never showed up. Maybe it was just one of those times when the enemy wasn't psychologically prepared to surrender."[222]

It became a responsibility of the MRB men to "get loudspeakers forward to where the enemy hear them. And at the same time set them in places where no one in the area gets killed when the Germans try to shut up the loudspeakers by shelling them."[223] Even after many months, the infantry officers would continue to question the effectiveness of loudspeaker appeals: guns, not words, were their weapons of choice. Arthur Hadley recognized this, even as he experienced terrible frustration when he was unable to get through to the colonel who was leading a regiment of the 29th Infantry Division in attacking a small group of buildings:

> I am close to certain I can get the Germans in those buildings to surrender with a loudspeaker broadcast. I have the speaker ready to be carried forward in the back of my jeep. But I cannot get permission from the colonel running the attack to make such a broadcast. [...] We loudspeaker personnel can pack up and leave. The infantry men have to remain and suffer the shelling. I try twice to persuade the colonel, but get a commanding brush off each time. I still believe I should have been able to make the broadcast.[224]

The earliest "hog calling" appeals were made from the sides or even from the seats of the Jeeps on which the loudspeakers were mounted. It was very quickly discovered that this made the loudspeakers and the men speaking into the microphone extremely vulnerable: the Germans simply aimed their shells at the Jeeps from which the appeal was coming. After a very short time, all three were separated: the two loudspeakers were run out a number of yards from the Jeep, and the microphone was also attached to a long wire, so that the speaker could address the enemy from the relative safety of a foxhole, where there was less likelihood of being fatally injured. Often the microphones were mouth microphones, strapped onto the speaker's face; these were considered optimal, since they eliminated extraneous noises. In spite of the safety precautions the men took, those who were involved in this work could suffer the consequences of having shells constantly landing

---

[222] Tom Wolf, "Novel 'Hog Calling' Offensive Crushes Morale of the Nazis."
[223] Arthur T. Hadley, *Heads or Tails*, 88.
[224] Arthur T. Hadley, *Heads or Tails*, 91.

near them. Some of them suffered concussions from the constant shelling, even when they were not directly hit.[225]

For broadcasts in conquered territories, the MRB men simply mounted loudspeakers on Jeeps or small tanks that they drove into French marketplaces and through the streets of the town. They had quickly learned that not all the French were pleased about the Allied invasion, the shellings and gun battles, and the destruction of their towns. Men from Sharpe interviewed the French civilians to gauge their animosity or joy over the Allied actions and used this information for propaganda directed to the French citizens. As Arthur Jaffe reported, "The loudspeaker units [...] distributed newspapers to the liberated French people,[226] set up local photographic displays of news pictures, and, with company French linguists as announcers, broadcast news and MG [military government] announcements from the main squares of the towns."[227] On July 4th, 2nd MRB Lieutenant Daniel Overton went on the air with a 400-watt mobile transmitter under the call sign of "Radio Cherbourg." These broadcasts continued until late August, when another transmitter took over the job.[228]

In the meantime, although he was essentially a radio producer, Sergeant Benno Frank was sent to help round up enemy soldiers hiding in Cherbourg and vicinity. In a less successful venture, two of the 2nd MRB men—intelligence officer Otto Schoeppler and loudspeaker announcer Hans Deppisch, who wore the disguise of a lieutenant colonel—set off, unarmed, on a white flag mission into an enemy pocket to negotiate surrender terms. They discovered, to their disappointment, that the Germans had already left the area.[229]

As the American army finally broke through at St. Lo, a radio reconnaissance team under Lieutenant Eugene Rotterman (2nd MRB company) moved into Brittany, to the site of the old Radio Rennes transmitter. Philip Pines's radio group drove their two trailer trucks to Thourie, about twenty miles south of Rennes. His group spent three to four days in Thourie, but couldn't use the modern 500 kilowatt station there, because it had been bombed and destroyed by the Germans.

---

[225] Author interview with Si Lewen, 26 July, 2013.
[226] First, *The Liberator*, then *La Presse Cherbourgeoise*, which went to a wider readership.
[227] Arthur H. Jaffe, *History, 2nd Mobile Radio Broadcasting Company*, 36.
[228] Arthur H. Jaffe, *History, 2nd Mobile Radio Broadcasting Company*, 37.
[229] Arthur H. Jaffe, *History, 2nd Mobile Radio Broadcasting Company*, 37.

Pines was placed on guard duty there, opposite the station. One night, when he was on night duty with Powerhouse Engineer Mike Arab, who was from Brooklyn and had a 50-caliber machine gun, they saw flashlights at a distance and Arab prepared to fire. Pines warned him not to, telling him "the people there could be French, or, if they were Germans, they would shoot back, and we are only seven or eight men."[230] The flashlights moved away, and Pines never did learn whether they belonged to friend or foe. Soon after this, the 2nd MRB's fixed radio section, under the direction of Lieutenant George Holbert, arrived with all the equipment necessary for setting up a fixed broadcast station there.

Pines was now moved from the broadcasting truck to the studio unit and placed with T/4 Albert Jeannotte, an MRB radio studio technician originally from French Canada. They left for Rennes and broadcast Radio Brittania (Bretagne); it went on the air on August 19th and was transmitted by wire to Thourie. In Rennes, Pines's team worked on broadcasts to the French civilians. General Marie-Pierre Koenig broadcast from there; he was the head of the French army on the continent, and Pines liked him. He was less fond of General Charles De Gaulle, who didn't bother to greet the radiomen or even to say thank you when the broadcast was over. "He thought he was only slightly below, or even above, God," Pines remembers.[231]

There was still fierce fighting for Brittany, and the MRB men were often in the thick of it. One day in Brest, then still a German submarine base, Si Lewen was scouting for a good spot from which to make his loudspeaker appeal to the Germans, when he came under enemy fire. For the first time, Lewen could actually see the enemy:

> Crouching in a doorway, I lifted my rifle and took aim at one German soldier firing from a window. But I was shaking and in cold sweat. [...] I did not so much as aim my rifle but point it, and the moment I pulled (not squeezed) the trigger, I bolted and ran. "What if, even with trembling fingers, I had shot him?" I wondered, after I stopped shaking. There were but a few other such incidences for the rest of my time at war, with however no improvement in my aim. Ultimately, long after the war, I thought that the worst part of war might not [be] to get killed but, possibly, to have killed someone, or so I try

---

[230] Author interview with Philip Pines, 15 Aug. 2013.
[231] Author interview with Philip Pines, 15 Aug. 2013.

to ease an uncertain conscience.[232]

On August 7, the 2nd MRB Company moved south to Periers to be closer to the headquarters of the 12th Army Group and to rejoin the 72nd Publicity Service Battalion.[233] At the same time, a small detachment of nine men, OSS and MRB members, was assigned to Lorient in order to lay radio siege to the German submarine base at Keroman. Twenty-eight thousand Germans were in the garrison, living in modern subterranean barracks and apartments; there were also thousands of soldiers from the routed German 7th Army, living in much less comfort and therefore more vulnerable to the appeals of the American broadcasters.[234] Hollywood screenwriter David Hertz, an OSS man, was teamed up with the opera director Benno Frank[235] and the Viennese actor Fred Lorenz[236], both of the 2nd MRB, as part of the broadcast team.

Lorient had been leveled by Allied bombers prior to the men's arrival; their task was, ostensibly, to soften German morale prior to an all-out Allied attack of the garrison. In reality, no Allied attack ever came, and "the only attack on the Germans was made by our nine-man team over the radio."[237] Lorient became a laboratory for testing the skills of the broadcasters, since the men had free hand to develop their sustained propaganda attacks against the Germans entrenched there. Much of the team's work was experimental. One of these experiments involved coordinating their radio propaganda with the firing of artillery leaflets. As Jaffe tells it,

---

[232] Si Lewen, *Reflections and Repercussions*," Chapter 18.
[233] Arthur H. Jaffe, *History, 2nd Mobile Radio Broadcasting Company*, 39.
[234] See David Hertz, "The Radio Siege of Lorient," 385.
[235] Frank was born in Mannheim, Germany, as the son of a Polish diplomat. In the early 1930s he directed the Schiller Opera at the Hamburg State Theater. In 1933 he emigrated to Palestine, where he established the Palestine Chamber Opera. Hampered by lack of funds, he moved to the United States in 1938, where he worked with the American League for Opera and the New York College of Music before moving to Philadelphia's Academy of Vocal Arts.
[236] Both before and after the war, Lorenz went by his birth name, Manfred Inger. In Vienna he was an ensemble member in a cabaret and in several prominent theaters. He fled Austria in 1938, going first to the Netherlands, then to the United States, where he performed in New York under the name of Fred Lorenz.
[237] David Hertz, "The Radio Siege of Lorient," 386.

A "game" was arranged with the artillery. One day, at a certain time, these [German 7th army] units were addressed by name and their members were told to go outside their buildings and five minutes later they would receive a message. Precisely, five minutes later, leaflet shells released the messages advising surrender. The ability of the Americans to do things like that impressed the German soldiers with their hopeless position more than words.[238]

In Lorient the nine-man broadcasting team developed highly effective programming that would be used to broader effect later in the war. They had the advantage of living in close quarters with the German prisoners; they ate, slept, and drank with them, and therefore, "We could measure more accurately the results of our broadcasts than perhaps any other radio station used in the war."[239]

Because of this, the broadcasters were able to address the enemy's most vital interests: "Every day we broadcast lists of Germans killed, wounded, and captured. This is the sort of information rarely available to an enemy during warfare. But even in our first broadcast we discovered that our best audience-building lay in reading the besieged men their personal mail, bags of which we had discovered when the garrison was first cut off."[240] Much of this mail from the home front had a despairing note, speaking of food shortages at home and the frequent bombings. In addition, a couple of deserters spoke on the radio each day, without, of course, indicating that they had willingly been taken prisoner by the Americans.

These prisoners gave the broadcasters detailed information about specific figures in the garrison; it was Benno Frank's idea to create a program feature from this called "Erlauschtes aus Lorient" (Things Heard from Lorient):

> Our best actor, Corporal Fred Lorenz, would work at the difficult job of mimicking a voice he had never heard by trying various nuances of tone until the deserter would say that Fred had hit the correct one. Next we would write dialogue we believed to be characteristic of the individual selected. [...] In the end we achieved a pretty close satirization of the characters in-

---

[238] Jaffe, *History, 2d Mobile Radio Broadcasting Co.*, 55.
[239] David Hertz, "The Radio Siege of Lorient," 386.
[240] David Hertz, "The Radio Siege of Lorient," 391.

side the garrison.[241]

These "characters" then addressed the war situation using gallows humor: "The Russians are fleeing from Russia—to Hungary, to Finland, to Germany. They don't like it in Russia. Well, who does?"[242]

Benno Frank himself assumed the role of a Captain Angers, a man who had served in the German army and was now an American army captain. Hertz said admiringly, "Benno was dynamically original in his attack on the enemy. He could sell anyone anything. [...] Over the radio Benno knew when to shout, when to whisper."[243] As "Captain Angers" Frank "spoke of everything near and dear to the heart of the German soldiers, of everything that concerned them." He also "attempted, with marked success, to acquaint the German soldier with the 'Yank.' He did this by commenting on the American way of life, the interesting but peculiar differences between German and American ways of doing things," and "he stressed the wholesome quality of democratic processes of government."[244] Frank's appeals were singularly effective; many of the deserters specifically asked to surrender to "Captain Angers." Indeed, the success of the Lorient operation was, in Jaffe's opinion, "due largely to the imagination and resources of T/3 [Benno] Frank."[245] His greatest strength "was his almost complete lack of orthodoxy. He had little time for the amenities of warfare that were prescribed by those who were tradition bound."[246]

Frank nearly got the entire mission in trouble when, without clearing his broadcast with his superiors, he announced over the radio one day: "Come over. If you don't like it here after a 30-hour trial period, you will be free to go back. On my honor, I will see to it that you are sent back! Ask for Captain Angers."[247]

The promise appeared to be a safe one; surely, no one who voluntarily deserted would desire to return to the besieged garrison. The day came, however, when an ardent Nazi named Fridolin Hopf was captured, and at the end of his 30-hour imprisonment he asked to be sent back to the German lines. Frank persuaded the Americans to let the

---

[241] David Hertz, "The Radio Siege of Lorient," 388
[242] David Hertz, "The Radio Siege of Lorient," 389.
[243] David Hertz, "The Radio Siege of Lorient," 387.
[244] W. E. D. [William E. Daughterty], "Benno Frank," 250.
[245] Jaffe, in conversation with the author, 19 Feb. 2014.
[246] W. E. D. [William E. Daugherty], "Benno Frank," 249.
[247] Cited in W. E. D. [William E. Daughterty], "Benno Frank," 250.

man leave, since much might be gained from the man's release. Hopf was loaded down with candy bars, cigarettes, gum, and canned food, and sent back to his unit. Frank made the most of this in the broadcasts that followed:

> He said that Hopf had not liked it in the American lines, but he had been the only dissatisfied customer among several hundred and his release was true evidence that he, Captain Angers, was a man who kept his word. Thereafter, Hopf was referred to as a sort of travel agent in Lorient for us. "Ask Hopf! You'll find him in Bunker No. 6, Barracks Four."[248]

Radio Lorient ceased operations on October 14. Since the broadcasting team's arrival in early August its audience had grown to several thousand, and the number of German deserters had also increased. Hertz recalled, "Our final score was something more than two hundred Germans for every member of our nine-man crew, although of course we never could be sure how many prisoners were trying to ingratiate themselves with flattery."[249] Their success was confirmed in a report that Major Ray K. Craft prepared for his superiors after the war; Craft noted that Lorient was "the sole example of a small transmitter in tactical radio propaganda" during the entire European conflict and that, "An average of 20 German soldiers each day deserted to the Americans during the period of this program, and after discontinuance of the program—when the radio team was called for another mission—almost no prisoners were taken."[250]

While the broadcasters were using all their ingenuity on the Germans to encourage their desertion from the safety of their fortified garrison in Lorient, the MRB pamphleteers were equally active in undermining German morale and bringing about the surrender of troops in Brittany. Sergeant Stefan Heym was asked to produce two pieces of propaganda that proved highly effective. The one was commissioned by Colonel Clifford R. Powell, Commanding Officer of the 12th Army Group's Psychological Warfare Service Battalion. Powell asked Heym to come up with an appeal that would make an entrenched group of

---

[248] David Hertz, "The Radio Siege of Lorient," 387-388.
[249] David Hertz, "The Radio Siege of Lorient," 392.
[250] Ray K. Craft, *Psychological Warfare in the European Theater of Operation*, 30.

Germans on the island of Cézembre surrender to the Americans, pointing out that, "As long as [the Germans] remain, the harbor of St. Malo is blocked, and we need the harbor, otherwise we have only Cherbourg and the facilities on Omaha and Utah Beach, and reinforcements must come for our advance [to Paris]."[251] The Allies had, throughout the summer, bombarded the island from land, sea, and air, even to the extent of using napalm bombs. Heym now came up with a tactical leaflet that featured a sketch representing the island as a direct target for an intense new attack by American bombers. He could say later, with justifiable pride,

> This was the only leaflet of the Second World War whose effectiveness could be observed immediately and in full measure [...], because mere hours after the airdrop the first white flags appeared at the openings in the battlements of Cézembre and the occupying troops, with many Poles among them, marched out, against the opposition of their officers.[252]

Heym also created a highly effective strategical leaflet featuring a photograph of "Joe Jones," a "typical" GI from Steubenville, Ohio, who stated that, "We don't believe in miracles. We believe in planes, cannons, grenades, tanks, and machines." Although "we want peace, calm, and order, and not just for 23 years," he could promise, that "whoever wants to be my enemy will quickly learn that I can also be a hard and relentless enemy. So hard and relentless, that my enemy will never forget me. Which Joe Jones do you want to meet?"[253]

Heym had been disturbed for some time by the ignorance of the German prisoners he questioned: "they know next to nothing about what's going on abroad, and they are extremely ill-informed about their own country and about the situation on the different fronts."[254] What if, he wondered, the MRB men produced a weekly newspaper in German that could be dropped into German territory and inform the Germans about the true war situation? Heym wrote a proposal to the

---

[251] Stefan Heym, *Nachruf*, 301.
[252] Stefan Heym, *Nachruf*, 303.
[253] Herbert A. Friedman and Franklin Prosser, "The United States PSYOP Organization in Europe During World War II," http://www.psywarrior.com/PSYOPOrgWW2.html, p. 45 of 58.
[254] Stefan Heym, *Nachruf*, 294.

PWD/SCHAEF urging the adoption of such a plan. Heym could not, with certainty, say that his proposal was the decisive factor in the rise of the German-language *Frontpost*, because, at about this same time, his old instructor Hans Habe showed up in Colombières, and immediately took over the layout of the new paper. The first issue was prepared in the operations tent in a field near St. Sauveur, in Normandy. Heym was assigned the task of overseeing the printing and delivery of the paper, and continued to monitor its production.

The first five issues were printed in Rennes. It was the stated objective of the paper to give the Germans "an impartial, objective presentation of world news which is not available through any German medium."[255] Propaganda was scrupulously avoided. Each issue consisted of one (and, later) two sheets, with the front page giving world and war news, and the others providing more popular items, like sports stories, crossword puzzles, and news from the home front. At first these papers were scattered by plane; later a smaller version of the paper, called *Feldpost*, was packed into artillery shells, 400 copies to a shell, and fired into German-held territories in France, the Netherlands, and Germany. During the 12th Army Group's rapid break through St. Lo and push to Paris, the paper appeared three times a week. By August 31st, Stefan Heym would be overseeing its printing in Paris.

In the meantime, Sergeant Albert Guerard of the 2nd MRB company had been serving as assistant to the British special agent Lieutenant George Langelaan. Langelaan was especially eager to get to Paris, and, as he and Guerard headed there, they met up with Ernest Hemingway in Rambouillet. Habe, who also met Hemingway in Rambouillet, recalled how he "lectured for hours in the lounge of the overcrowded little hotel about his adventures during the capture of Rambouillet."[256] Hemingway, Langelaan, and Habe were all determined to be the first to enter Paris. On August 24th, the rumor spread that fighting was going on in the streets of Paris and that French and U.S. advanced units had entered the city from the south. All three men set out in Jeeps. Langelaan beat Hemingway by making a "highly improper nighttime excursion into Paris" and engaging in a "one-car liberation of the Porte de St. Cloud" the next morning. It was an action that could have had Langelaan courtmartialed—and Guerard with him, had it become

---

[255] *PWB Combat Team...*, 51.
[256] Hans Habe, *All My Sins*, 343.

known.[257] Meanwhile, Habe, Major Patrick Dolan of the OSS, and their driver "resorted to the old soldier's dodge of 'looking for one's unit' and drove their Jeep straight for Paris." They arrived one day before the occupying German garrison surrendered and the French General Jacques Leclerc entered the city in triumph. Habe said that he entered Paris early "for [his wife] Eleanor's sake."[258] He was motivated, he said, to go and "liberate" Eleanor's Parisian house and contents by "a bad conscience. I had lied to her [about my heritage]: I was a Jew, not a nobleman. At least I must be a hero."[259] Habe not only liberated the home, but also drove to the Champs Élysées, where he forced one of France's great designers to open her establishment and to sell him four dresses that he could send to his wife.

The next day, fifty of the MRB men entered Paris and participated enthusiastically in the rewards of a grateful city. They were given rooms in the Hotel Scribe; Hanuš Burger shared a room there with Habe:

> We moved in at about five in the afternoon. In a few minutes the short Rue Scribe had been transformed into an ambulatory bordello. The olive-green army vehicles were parked bumper to bumper, the bright clothes of the enthusiastic Parisian girls fluttered around among them, rhythmic American music resounded from the loudspeaker wagon at full volume, wine and cognac bottles passed from mouth to mouth, and soon there was hardly a member of the unit who was not already well provided for in all respects.
>
> Habe and I looked out on the wide inner courtyard. In all the windows across from us officers were standing and waving and toasting each other; each one had a girl in his arm, not all of them were still dressed, people were swaying to the beat of the music that rang up from below, they drank champagne, kissed one another, and celebrated liberation.[260]

Habe and Burger had to go by foot to a broadcast station that was

---

[257] Albert Guerard, *The Touch of Time*, 75.
[258] Hans Habe, *All My Sins*, 343.
[259] Hans Habe, *All My Sins*, 345.
[260] Hanuš Burger, *Der Frühling war es wert*, 182. In his novel *The Crusaders* (1948) Stefan Heym portrays the liberation of Paris and the darker side of these celebrations.

still intact in a distant corner of the city. There Habe broadcast to the German soldiers: "Paris has freed itself."[261]

The next day, General Charles De Gaulle entered Paris. Habe and Burger set out in a Jeep to watch the parade, but were held up on the Place de la Concorde because of the mobs that had already gathered there. Suddenly, gunfire erupted from one of the rooftops. Everyone reacted in panic, since the crowds had no place on the square where they could flee for protection.

> Habe reacted in a strange way that was unique to him. It was a bit theatrical, quixotic, perhaps a little ridiculous. But above all, it was, in these minutes, unexpectedly expedient.
>
> He stood up, drew his pistol from his belt, braced his left hand against his hip and fired in the direction of the rooftop, where the tiny, scarcely visible snipers were crouched behind their machine guns. It was completely senseless. His pistol could not reach that far under any circumstances. But he achieved that which he had probably intended. The people around us, who had sought insufficient cover behind our jeep, watched dumbfoundedly as the crazy American officer, who was standing with his legs apart in his open jeep, fired off all the ammunition in his pistol. The panic, at least from those within sight of our vehicle, abated.
>
> By then the men in their tanks had their guns directed at the opposing roof. Their salvos crashed, the capitals of the Greek columns splintered, and the horrific episode was over.[262]

Some of the MRB men were native Frenchmen, and they were now returning "home" to Paris; others had spent time in Paris as students or as refugees, long before the outbreak of the war. Now they were able to look up their former homes, student haunts, and restaurants. For these soldiers, the city's liberation meant more than just another battle won. It felt like the war was essentially over. But, while some men, like Leon Edel, were left behind in Paris to monitor the French press, most were ordered out, to Luxembourg and to Verdun, where they would be joined by the newly-arrived members of the 4th and 5th MRB companies.

---

[261] Hanuš Burger, *Der Frühling war es wert*, 182.
[262] Hanuš Burger, *Der Frühling war es wert*, 184.

Chapter 5

Luxembourg

> *The little Grand Duchy was of no strategic significance; its only valuable military objective was the transmitter tower of Junglinster. It was the highest transmitter in the world and one of the most powerful radio stations in Europe. [...] Radio Luxembourg fell into our hands unscathed.*
>
> *For the next seven months I was in charge of the German department of "Radio Free Luxembourg" and the "Voice of the U.S. Twelfth Army Group."*[263]

On September 10, 1944, the Allied forces retook the Grand Duchy of Luxembourg and entered the capital city. The Germans retreated with scarcely a fight. Bert Anger, Samson Knoll, and William Sailer of the 2nd MRB had been sent forward to assist in securing the radio station. On September 12 the station's transmitters were captured by American infantry and a force of armored vehicles; although holes had been shot in the transmitter tubes, a station engineer dug up a spare set of tubes that he had buried on the station grounds some four years earlier. The studios themselves were unharmed.

Control of the Luxembourg facilities was given to SHAEF as "the voice of the Supreme Headquarters Allied Expeditionary Force acting on behalf of the United States, Britain, France, Belgium and Luxembourg." Prior to its takeover by the U.S. Army, the Germans had used the station to broadcast propaganda by English-language announcers generically known as "Lord Haw-Haw."[264] Now, however, the Psychological Warfare Branch used the facilities for its own propaganda, with much of it being spoken by Camp Sharpe men and broadcast in German.

Lt. Colonel Sam Rosenbaum was Commanding Officer of the Ra-

---

[263] Hans Habe, *All My Sins*, 346, 347.

[264] The original Lord Haw-Haw was William Joyce; he had been brought up in Ireland, moved to Germany in 1939, and began broadcasting to England a few weeks after the beginning of the war. He acquired his soubriquet because of his "pseudo-cultured accents" and the "wry humor" of his broadcasts. See M. J., "William Joyce, Propagandist of Treason," 237.

dio Luxembourg Detachment, working under the direction of the PWD/SHAEF director, Brig. General Robert A. McClure, and Colonel William S. Paley of the OWI (Office of War Information). But it was Captain Hans Habe who was given the task of restoring programming to the German-speaking populations of Europe. Working under military supervision from the front and political supervision from Paris, and with the full support of his superior, Colonel Clifford R. Powell, Hans Habe stated proudly that he "shaped Radio Luxembourg into one of the most successful instruments of psychological warfare."[265] The nine-man team from Lorient was called to the station; these men had gained the expertise necessary for creating programming that had already proven itself in Brittany. Habe called in other men from the 2nd and 3rd MRB companies, including Stefan Heym, Peter Wyden, and Jules Bond, while Captain Joseph Goularte brought in a larger number of men from the 4th MRB company, among them Robert Addis, Roger Brett, Robert Breuer, Joseph Eaton,[266] Walter Kohner, Ernest Loewenbein, Fred Perutz, and Joseph Wechsberg. They joined technicians and staff members from the OWI in putting out four propaganda programs each day as well as daily features. Stefan Heym recalls that the German section was an odd group. "The central core of those who did the actual work were writers and journalists, university professors and students of German literature, refugees from Germany and Austria, most of whom had become naturalized citizens of the United States only recently."[267] Few, other than the men from Lorient, had any experience in radio work; "there is no time for training and who should teach the art of it, anyway? The programming must begin over night, the announcers are waiting at their microphones. [...] Only practice can reveal how it is done."[268] By the end of September they were able to air their first program. For its theme music, music director Ernest Loewenbein selected Gustav Holst's "The Planets."[269]

The MRB men made no effort to hide the fact that their broadcasts were coming from a station controlled by the American army, but they got a wide airing in the German-held territories simply by report-

---

[265] Hans Habe, *All My Sins*, 347.
[266] Joseph Eaton's birth name was Josef Wechsler.
[267] Stefan Heym, *Nachruf*, 309.
[268] Stefan Heym, *Nachruf*, 310.
[269] Author interview with Fred Perutz, 13 Oct. 2013.

ing the truth about the war situation. German families listened to the station for news about family members fighting at the Allied front. As at Lorient, the announcers read off the names of Germans who had been captured in the most recent fighting at each of their news broadcasts; as in Lorient, they also broadcast feature programming, including short skits and plays. Two "characters" who appeared regularly in these skits were a Corporal Tom Jones, an all-American GI who spoke German with a markedly American accent, and Colonel Thompson, with less of an American accent, but with a deep, authoritative voice. Corporal Jones spoke to the common German soldier as a man who shared their concerns; the "colonel" spoke to the higher officers about the hopeless situation in which the German troops now found themselves.

The contrast between the two speakers, who appeared in the same program, was marked. On February 1, 1945, for example, Colonel Thompson addressed the issue of German strategy regarding time and space. It was, he stated, German policy to sacrifice space (i.e., territory) in order to gain time, time to regroup and to bring in supplies and fresh recruits. This had been a sensible approach in the campaigns of 1866, 1870, and even 1939. But in the winter of 1944 the German general staff "had given up so much space that a continuation of this policy would have endangered the [German] heartland." And that policy certainly made no sense in 1945. One should ask, instead, why the general staff was even trying to win time.[270]

> Time gives Germany neither men nor material [now], since Germany's factories are being occupied or destroyed. Time can't give Germany the secret weapon, either, since, until now, it has not slowed the advance of the Allies by a single day. The time that Germany's leadership has given the German people is time to suffer, time to be destroyed, time to die.
> Goodbye!

There was a short pause, followed by a voice, "Hello, Tom!," and Tom's reply, "Hello, boys!" A soldier asks, "What's new?" and Tom begins talking about Hitler's speech about the latest assassination attempt on his life.[271] Tom then remarks,

---

[270] Stefan Heym, *Reden an den Feind*, 287.
[271] Stefan Heym, *Reden an den Feind*, 288.

> Every soldier in this war has experienced a near-death experience. I myself have a piece of shrapnel in my arm—and it's only a few centimeters from my heart, which is considerably closer than the meter and a half which supposedly brought Hitler so close to his demise.
>
> But I don't use this as an excuse to stand up and say that I have the right to sacrifice millions of people. I believe that one should be humble before God and that one should not use the name of the Almighty for one's personal aims.[272]

The actor playing the role of "Tom Jones" described his broadcasting role this way:

> Tom spoke with an atrocious American accent, which was all to the good; there was no suspicion that he was a German-born turncoat. He told human-interest anecdotes in a simple and even naive way, which left him free of the taint of cleverness, sharp dealing or underhanded needling. And he finished off each night's stint with a joke—an anti-Nazi joke, to be sure, but still something you could laugh at and pass on to a neighbor or fellow-soldier. As [one] can see from the comments of [Prisoners of War] and others, the joke was a great factor in Tom's appeal.[273]

Just as Stefan Heym had created leaflets featuring the American-German GI "Joe Jones," he now wrote many of these skits for "Tom." He also utilized, verbatim, texts from his own propaganda leaflets as broadcasting material.[274] And he continued to oversee the publication of the *Frontpost*, which was now being printed in Luxembourg,[275] and

---

[272] Stefan Heym, *Reden an den Feind*, 289.
[273] Richard F. Hanser, cited in Daniel Lerner, *Psychological Warfare against Nazi Germany*, 205.
[274] Heym published seventy of the pieces that he wrote for Radio Luxembourg under the title *Reden an den Feind* (Speeches to the Enemy, 1986). Several of these are identical to leaflets appealing to specific units to surrender.
[275] At the same time, Heym's colleague Peter Wyden was producing a miniature version of *Frontpost* called *Feldpost*, which could be distributed by artillery shells rather than by bombs.

to incorporate some of its articles into the broadcasting.[276]

As at Lorient, one of Radio Luxembourg's most popular, recurring programs was called "Letters That Were Never Received." These letters were culled from those found in abandoned mail sacks in the towns conquered by the Allies. Letters addressed both to and from the home front were now read aloud on the air.[277] Walter Kohner recalled that not all the radio shows from Luxembourg were directed to German territories:

> Our news team wrote and translated the daily news and bulletins into German, French, Italian, Russian, Czech and Dutch.[278] Different announcers were broadcasting around the clock. I transmitted the news in German three times daily. There were musical interludes during the newsbreaks. Local news was broadcast in Luxembourgoise, a melange of French and German. Twice weekly the local string orchestra gave a live performance.[279]

For its musical selections, the station made it a point to give special emphasis to the music of composers who were banned by the Nazis.[280]

The day-to-day calm of the Luxembourg radio station was, however, suddenly shattered in mid-December. Habe related,

> I had calmly gone to bed on December 15, but was woken during the early hours of the morning with the news that the Wehrmacht was within a mile and a half of Luxembourg and within about half a mile of our transmitter towers of Junglinster. Between us and Sepp Dietrich's armoured units[281] was nothing but a company of hastily collected military policemen, radio engineers, and cooks.

---

[276] See Ray K. Craft, *Psychological Warfare in the European Theater of Operation*, 22.
[277] Author interview with Fred Perutz, 28 Sept. 2013.
[278] Also Flemish, Polish, Italian, and English. See Daniel Lerner, *Psychological Warfare against Nazi Germany*, 225.
[279] Hanna and Walter Kohner, with Frederick Kohner, *Hanna and Walter: A Love Story*, 166.
[280] Daniel Lerner, *Psychological Warfare against Nazi Germany*, 225.
[281] Josef "Sepp" Dietrich was an SS general in command of the newly created 6th Panzer Army.

The following days were tense:

> Although Luxembourg was of no strategic importance, and although the German offensive was rapidly developing in the direction of Liège, where the Wehrmacht was hoping to capture the vast petrol dumps of the U.S. and British forces, the entire U.S. General Staff was assembled in the Luxembourg General Post Office, and it seemed unbelievable that the Germans would miss the opportunity of taking the city.
>
> [...] Under protest, on superior orders, we had removed the transmitter valves from the towers, and therefore had to suspend our transmissions abruptly.[282]

The sudden loss of the radio broadcasts caused chaos in Luxembourg and no little worry back home. Fred Perutz remembers that his wife, like many others, heard about the sudden silencing of Radio Luxembourg and was very much afraid that her husband had been killed or captured.[283]

And the danger was very real, in part because of a maneuver by the German SS called *Operation Greif*, or "Gryphon." This was a plot to send Germans who spoke nearly accent-free English behind the Allied lines in British and U.S. army uniforms and in captured Allied Jeeps. Their purpose was to create confusion and delay the Allied advance towards the Rhine River.

The Germans did not have enough Allied equipment to make this offensive a serious threat, except among the German-born MRB men. This threat increased after it was rumored that some hundred SS men in American uniforms had penetrated into Luxembourg. Security was beefed up in the capital, and measures were taken to arrest anyone suspected of having entered into Luxembourg from the German lines. Habe reported that "I was myself arrested a few times on suspicion of being a German parachutist."[284]

Whenever one of the foreign-born MRB soldiers was halted, he had to "prove" that he was American. The men from Sharpe had been thoroughly trained in German ways, but not in American ones, and many had had little time to pick up the cultural references now

---

[282] Hans Habe, *All My Sins*, 348..
[283] Author interview with Fred Perutz, 28. Sept. 2013.
[284] Hans Habe, *All My Sins*, 349.

thrown at them by the arresting MPs. Igor Cassini (5th MRB) was halted and could not answer any of the questions an MP put to him about American football games and players:

> So there we were, one American ready to kill another (with all the best intentions) because I could not tell a tackle from a back. Something must have given him pause that I was on the level, perhaps my total loss at faking it. The sarge called over a lieutenant:
> "Igor Cassini... Cassini," the lieutenant said. "Are you that Washington columnist? I've read some of your stuff." (Give that man a lifetime subscription.)[285]

Walter Kohner remembered the near arrest of a non-celebrity Sharpe boy:

> One evening a member of my [4th MRB] company, Corporal [Ernest] Loewenbein, a musician of studious appearance from Berlin, accompanied a German prisoner to headquarters for interrogation. They spoke English—the German almost perfectly, Loewenbein with a heavy accent. A tough MP stopped them. He listened to Loewenbein suspiciously and asked him, "How many homers did Babe Ruth hit?" Loewenbein was stumped. "What's the name of Li'l Abner's girlfriend?" Loewenbein stared uncomfortably at the sergeant. For a moment it was touch-and-go for Loewenbein. Only when the sergeant was about to nail him with the third question "Who's Dr Pepper?," did Loewenbein smile and answer in his most fastidious manner, "Sergeant, it is not *who* is Dr Pepper—but *what* is Dr Pepper!" The sergeant laughed and let them pass.[286]

The threat to the foreign-born MRB men became so serious for a time, that none of them dared to go out onto the streets of Luxembourg without being accompanied by a native-born American.[287]

Transmissions were resumed, however, in spite of the outbursts of

---

[285] Igor Cassini, *I'd do it all over again*, 101.
[286] Hanna and Walter Kohner, with Frederick Kohner, *Hanna and Walter: A Love Story*, 167-168.
[287] Author interview with Fred Perutz, 13 Oct. 2013.

rifle shots and the explosions of shells. Habe gave his men the option of leaving the radio station and seeking safety further back from the fighting, but all of them declared themselves willing to stay. Kohner recalled: "We celebrated part of Christmas in the basement of Radio Luxembourg, but broadcasting never stopped. We wore steel helmets and kept our guns near our microphones."[288] The German section had been announcing for several months that it would, as part of its Christmas programming, allow 1,000 prisoners of war to speak directly to their families. The mobile radio units had traveled to various prisoner of war camps to make recordings of these Christmas greetings. They were played on Christmas day.[289] Soon after Christmas, the Germans were forced back, and Luxembourg remained a safe haven for future broadcasting.

During these months of "white" broadcasting, Radio Luxembourg shared air-time with "black" programming; this went out late at night on a German wavelength, and purported to come from a Rhineland station inside of Germany. The men working with the daytime, "white" programming, looked down a bit on "Luxembourg Operation" as a purveyor of dirty tricks. Stefan Heym questioned how "secret" this American operation actually was: "The station, whose location was supposed to be super secret, began its broadcasts immediately after the Luxembourg station bade its listeners good night, and had almost the same wave length as our 1313 [theirs was 1212]."[290]

Nevertheless, "Twelve Twelve," or "Operation Annie," would prove to be a highly effective tool of military propaganda, and some of the Camp Sharpe graduates were essential to its success. Hanuš Burger, Allesandro Frank, Curt Jellin (2nd MRB company) and Walter Henschel (3rd) transferred over to "Operation Annie," joining forces with staffing from the Office of War Information and the Office of Strategic Services. The Lorient group was also part of this operation. Once again, Viennese actor Fred Lorenz used his talents of mimicry to play numerous on-air roles, while opera director Benno Frank served as the station's main speaker. This time, however, Frank dropped the pretense of being a former German serving as captain in the American army; he was, instead, a German army officer retired from active ser-

---

[288] Hanna and Walter Kohner, with Frederick Kohner, *Hanna and Walter: A Love Story*, 168.
[289] See Interview with Joseph Eaton by Judith Cohen, 1 Aug. 2010, 43-44.
[290] Stefan Heym, *Nachruf*, 317.

vice because of wounds.[291] Hanuš Burger said of Frank's performances:

> Benno was really the voice of 1212. It was full, rasping, mature and it spoke with an unmistakable Rhine-Hessian accent. As many interrogations with military and civilian prisoners later revealed, "You had to believe what he was saying." Benno held the program together, whetted the audience's appetite for coming attractions, gave the musical program unity and took over all those special features which needed the authority of a man of experience and integrity.[292]

Annie's headquarters were located in a villa that had formerly belonged to a high Nazi official, and its rooms were filled with Nazi memorabilia: flags, busts of Hitler, gilded swastikas, and SS shields. The men kept these Nazi symbols around them in order to maintain the illusion of operating an enemy radio station.[293]

> At 9, every night, Maj. Patrick Dolan, who was in charge of the operation and Alfred Toombs, chief of intelligence, arrived from the inner sanctum of the war room and behind closed doors drew the top secret picture of the past and the coming day. Only the military writers were admitted to these briefings. They were told the truth and nothing but the truth. A short conference on the slant of the night's news followed.[294]

Unlike the "degenerate" composers played on the "white" programming from Luxembourg, Annie featured German folk-songs and Viennese waltzes. Its theme song was "Es liegt eine Krone tief im Rhein" (There lies a crown, deep in the Rhine), which is a lesser known folksong quite in keeping with broadcasts that allegedly came from the Rhineland. The writers and announcers of Annie sought to influence the Germans by pretending to be "warmly pro-German, sadly and desperately honest and by creating reports that were not always truthful."[295] They did this by claiming to be a "group of SS dissidents who decided that the Fuehrer needed protection from [his] corrupt

---

[291] Brewster Morgan, "Operation Annie," 124.
[292] H. H. Burger, "Operation Annie: Now It Can Be Told," 13.
[293] Brewster Morgan, "Operation Annie," 19.
[294] H. H. Burger, "Operation Annie: Now It Can Be Told," 13.
[295] "Radio: Operation Annie," *TIME Magazine*, 25 Feb. 1946.

subordinates."[296] This was a clever ruse: the men in intelligence knew that many of their German listeners remained loyal to Hitler, despite their loathing of German atrocities and their own personal war losses. Annie broadcast for four-and-a-half hours each night. Programming included reports on both the front line and at home, all from the German perspective.

Annie's first task as a "black" operation was to gain credibility—and a widespread German audience—by giving only accurate news reports. As part of their subterfuge, they worked tirelessly to give "an eyewitness account of an Allied air raid [as] seen on the ground, not from the air."[297] By using the latest aerial photographs of Allied bombings, and comparing these with earlier photographs, with maps and telephone books, and through interrogation of captured locals, the men were able to create highly accurate reports for their broadcasts about the damage that was being done to German cities, simply by naming specific businesses and homes that had suffered in the latest bombings.

Once full credibility had been created, and more and more Nazis accepted her authenticity, Annie became bolder:

> Soon, she appealed for help from other sectors to rescue surrounded party leaders. More men & equipment were thus lured into capture. On other occasions, Annie would innocently report "facts" that troubled civilians. Example: the Reich's cartographical institute, said Annie, was short of maps numbered 315 to 318; they were badly needed for national defense. Why, the Germans asked themselves, did the high command need maps of Westphalia, still 300 miles inside the Reich? [...]
> Annie's biggest day came soon after the Remagen bridge was taken. Another Allied force had secured a bridgehead near Andernach. Between these two points, Nazi troops in the Eifel mountains had ample room for retreat. Yet because Annie hinted that there was only one way out, most of the remaining Wehrmacht marched right into an Allied ambush.[298]

---

[296] Interview with Joseph Eaton by Judith Cohen, United States Holocaust Memorial Museum, 1 Aug. 2010, 41.
[297] Brewster Morgan, "Operation Annie," 19.
[298] "Radio: Operation Annie," *TIME Magazine*, 25 Feb. 1946.

As the Allied forces moved into the Rhineland, Operation Annie increased its deceptions:

> Annie gave the same sort of detailed battle news that she had been broadcasting with proved accuracy for months. But when the 7th Army started to make sharp progress through the Siegfried Line, Annie reported the American forces as being repulsed or held without gain. When the truth had to be admitted, Annie blamed misguided informants who endeavored to conceal the truth.[299]

As the Allies gained more and more territory in Germany, it became increasingly difficult for Annie to maintain the illusion that it was broadcasting from the Rhineland. The men began to add a tone of urgency to their broadcasts, and to report that they were under direct attack from the Americans, and might have to run: "Our chief speaker, Sgt. – later Lt. – Benno Frank, grew huskier by the hour. He mourned the destruction of the lovely Rhineland, and frankly refused to criticize the townspeople who, in the face of inevitable disaster, hung white flags from their windows."[300]

When this pretense could no longer be maintained, Generals Eisenhower and Bradley decided that Annie should "escape from her hide-out, set up business beyond the Rhine and start a German revolution against the Nazis." On Friday, April 6th, the strains of Wagner's *Twilight of the Gods* replaced the usual Rhenish folk-song, and Benno Frank spoke "in a voice husky with emotion, but resolute in purpose." He said:

> Germany, our fatherland, bleeds from a thousand wounds, and for Germany bleed our hearts. In the long history of our people, replete with glory and with greatness, with trials and tribulations, there has never been a moment when the life of the German nation was so seriously at stake. Our cities, testimonials to a proud past, fall now into ruins; our fathers, our sons, our husbands, warrantors of Germany's future, lie cold on the battlefield.
>
> With incomparable courage, our people have accepted their sacrifices—fighting, working, hoping—hoping for victory.

---

[299] Brewster Morgan, "Operation Annie," 122.
[300] Brewster Morgan, "Operation Annie," 122.

> We, too, had hoped, up to the very last. If we were assailed by doubts, we have clung stoutly to the belief that the valor of our troops, the sorrows and sacrifices of our men and women, could not have been in vain.
> [...] Today we know that this hopeless war is lost. Our lines of defense are shattered. Without pity or hindrance, enemy planes destroy our homes and our factories. The final crisis is upon us. [...]
> Only by courageous action can Germany draw back from the abyss. In cities throughout the Reich innumerable people have come together in groups under the banner of a New Germany. With them we are resolved to fight for immediate peace. Twelve twelve will give guidance to their groups. Twelve twelve summons every German [...] to join one of these groups [...].[301]

Brewster Morgan, the OWI's chief of broadcasting, remarked that Benno Frank's appeal that night was, in style and delivery, "the finest radio performance I have ever heard." The Annie staff was "stunned into silence," and, weeks later captured Germans "wept as they spoke of it. On that April Friday the Annie staff had hit some kind of a bullseye."[302]

Annie's goal was now to persuade Germany's fortified towns to surrender en masse, by turning the apathy of German civilians into a firm resolve to end the war. They would do this by making the imaginary "New Germany" movement seem real to the Germans. It is, of course, hard to determine how big a part these broadcasts played in the final conquest of Germany, but the men of Operation Annie did learn that their broadcasts actually inspired the development of several real "New Germany" groups in the unconquered territories.

Soon, however, the conquest of Germany had proceeded so far that Annie's broadcasts were no longer needed. On April 25th, at two thirty in the morning, the men practiced a final deception:

> For several days, the crew [had] sadly reported approaching Yanks. On the fatal night, grave messages came over 1212 with disturbing frequency. Suddenly the broadcast was interrupted by excited voices, a scuffle in the outer room, shouts

---

[301] Brewster Morgan, "Operation Annie," 123.
[302] Brewster Morgan, "Operation Annie," 123.

and shots. The hated Allies were seizing the transmitter! "Put on the record, the RECORD!," a German voice [Benno Frank] shouted. And as Annie began, so she died, with [its] reedy, recorded Rhenish [theme song].[303]

Although "Operation Annie" ceased operations on April 25th, Habe's German section would continue its work at Radio Luxembourg, unchallenged, through V-E-Day in May 1945. From then until November the station remained under American control. It relayed programs from the Voice of America, but Habe's old German section also continued producing news reports and original programming under the call sign of "The United Nations Sender." Walter Kohner reported:

> Even though the war in Europe was over, the station's schedule remained the same. News and bulletins focused on the war in the Far East. For one hour every day we broadcast lists of names of foreign workers who had been liberated by Allied forces and were waiting to be repatriated, and names of German POWs. On rare occasions we interviewed high-ranking German officers now prisoners of war.[304]

The men from Sharpe continued this programming until the station was handed back to the Grand Duchy of Luxembourg in November 1945. Pierre Dupong, Prime Minister of Luxembourg, then awarded the men at the station medals for services rendered to the State. This was a pleasant surprise, because winning the medal gave each of the men 5 points toward the 85 points they would have to collect in order to win discharge from the army.[305]

---

[303] "Radio: Operation Annie," *TIME Magazine*, 25 Feb. 1946.
[304] Hanna and Walter Kohner, with Frederick Kohner, *Hanna and Walter*, 194.
[305] Author interview with Fred Perutz, 28 Sept. 2013. Soldiers were given one point for each month served and five points for each medal.

Berlin native Gunter Kosse trained as a Ranger for intelligence service behind German lines. (Courtesy of G. Kosse)

As principal instructor at Camp Sharpe, Hans Habe was an odd blend of industry and theatricality. (Frederick Fell)

The propaganda class of the 4th MRB Company, as photographed at Camp Sharpe. From left to right. Front row: #1 Louis DeMilhau, #4 Paul Joachim Brand, #5 Herbert Schlesinger; Second row: #3 Joseph Wechsberg, #4 Albert G. Rosenberg, #5 Alexandre Behr, #6 Hans Habe, #8 Peter Hart, #9 Fred Perutz, #10 Albert Orbaan; Third row: #1 Max Logan, #2 Ernest S. Biberfeld, #5 Paul F. Gunther, #6 Walter Kohner, #7 Adolph E. Meier; Back row: #3 Elmer J. Theriault, #4 Francis D. Perkins, #8 Gary Babin, #10 Arthur Bardos, #11 Igor Cassini, #13 John Simon, #14 Victor Lasky. (Courtesy of Bo Ramsey)

Hanuš Burger of the 2ⁿᵈ MRB Company was a documentary filmmaker from Czechoslovakia. Photograph by J. Malan Heslop. (National Archives and Records Administration)

Igor Cassini, of Russian and Italian extraction, was not cut out for military duty, despite his popularity with his fellow soldiers. (From private collection)

The printing section of the 2nd MRB Company. From left to right: Thomas Metcalf, Russel Warren, Edward Bardgett, William Locke, Gene Seitz, Louis Mellitz, and Sarkis Phillian. (National Archives and Records Administration)

William Windsor checks the mobile Webendorfer offset press while printing leaflets for the front. Photograph by J. Malan Heslop. (National Archives and Records Administration)

Two escaped Russians who were doing forced labor on the heavy gun emplacements near Cherbourg, give information to Otto Schoeppler (far left), Robert Segal, and Hanuš Burger (far right). Photograph by Lt. Collier. (U.S. Signal Corps photo, National Archives and Records Administration)

Si Lewen, 3rd MRB Company, instructed German soldiers on how to surrender. (Courtesy of Si Lewen)

Hans Deppisch, one of his company's most successful "hog callers," is shown here with a mouth microphone and portable loudspeaker. Lieutenant Colonel Gordon Eyler, commanding officer of an infantry battalion, stands behind him. (War Pool Photo, National Archives and Records Administration)

Twenty minutes after a broadcast from the Allied lines, German prisoners come in to surrender at Balue (near St. Malo, Brittany). (War Pool Photo, National Archives and Records Administration)

Arthur Jaffe assumed command of the 2ⁿᵈ MRB Company and wrote its history. Photograph by Sgt. Garrett. (Courtesy of Arthur Jaffe)

Having loaded 105 mm shells with the German soldiers' newspaper "Feldpost," Rudolf Moskovits and Rudy Cook, both of the 2nd MRB Company, place the projectiles in their cases, along with an English translation of the material contained in it. Photograph by J. Malan Heslop. (Brigham Young University, Harold B. Lee Library, L. Tom Perry Special Collections)

Members of a U.S. field artillery unit cover their ears against the noise of their 105 mm gun, from which they have just fired a shell containing information leaflets. (U.S. Signal Corps Photo, National Archives and Records Administration)

A loudspeaker is set up in the window of a factory and beamed at the enemy just a short distance away. (National Archives and Records Administration)

Daniel Overton, 2ⁿᵈ MRB, handles the controls and Imlay Watts (BBC) checks the script as a French civilian, a prisoner of the Germans for more than a year and a half, stands at the microphone of the first Radio Cherbourg. Photograph by Weston Haynes. (PWD-OWI Staff Photo, National Archives and Records Administration)

In his Luxembourg office Stefan Heym works on the four-page Allied newspaper "Frontpost" that is printed in German and dropped by bomber to enemy troops. Photograph by Harold W. King. (U.S. Army Signal Corps, National Archives and Records Administration)

Left to right, Fred Lorenz, David Hertz, and Benno Frank broadcast for "Operation Annie" in Luxembourg. Photograph by J. Malan Heslop. (Brigham Young University, Harold B. Lee Library, L. Tom Perry Special Collections)

Walter Reichenbach, 2nd MRB Company, interrogates German prisoner Gunther Enger in Belgium in December 1944. Photograph by J. Malan Heslop. (National Archives and Records Administration)

Eddie Amicone, 2nd MRB Company, served as a driver for "Hog Calling" runs in Europe. (Courtesy of E. Amicone)

Edward Alexander, 5ᵗʰ MRB Company, analyzed German propaganda materials at Twelfth Army Headquarters in Verdun, in order to gauge the morale of the enemy. (Courtesy of E. Alexander)

Loudspeaker on an American M5 light tank is used to tell the people of Zerbst, Germany, that the town has fallen, and to order the end of resistance. Photo by Pfc. R. Gerick. (National Archives and Records Administration)

Gaston Pender, 4th MRB Company, felt that the infantrymen were the real heroes of the war. (Courtesy of Bo Ramsey)

American soldiers cheer as the skies clear and American planes can begin to provide air cover during the Battle of the Bulge. To the far right: Eddie Amicone. (Courtesy of E. Amicone)

BBC newscaster Stanley Maxted holds a microphone prior to making a broadcast on January 1, 1945, from a "doghouse" radio studio manned by Louis Muhlbauer (standing) and Philip Pines. (Corbis Images)

Brigadier General Charles Doran congratulates Otto Schoeppler in Verdun after awarding him the Bronze Star for meritorious achievement against the enemy. Photograph by W. E. Williams. (National Archives and Records Administration)

Bert Anger and an unidentified Russian meet at the Elbe River, in Torgau. (Courtesy of Helen Anger)

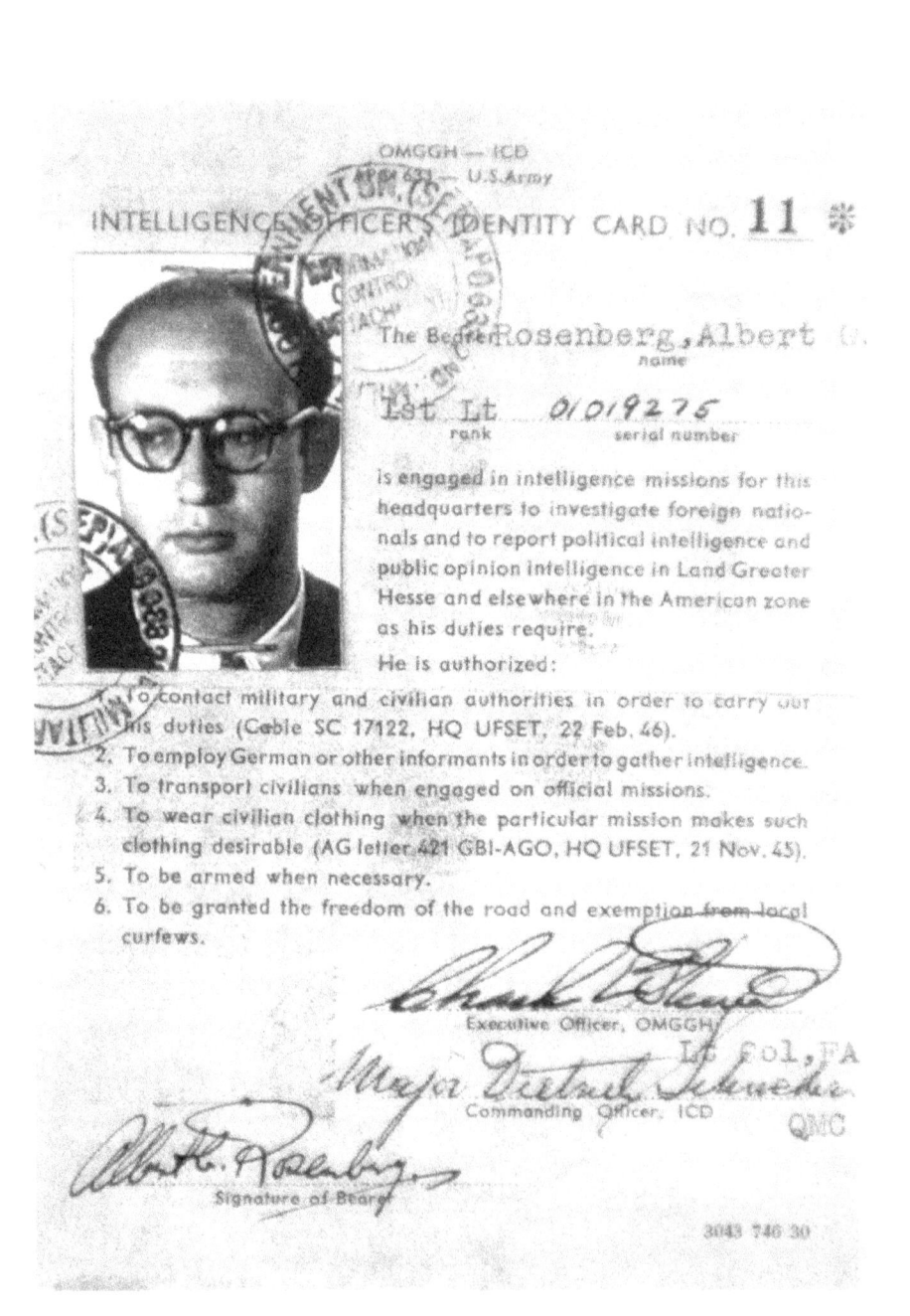

Albert G. Rosenberg's ICD identification card. (El Paso Times)

Citizens of Weimar are shown the carnage of Buchenwald. (National Archives and Records Administration)

A scene at Thekla, photographed by Bert Anger. (Courtesy of Otto Schoeppler)

Fred Perutz, 4ᵗʰ MRB Company, was operated on by an SS surgeon. (Courtesy of F. Perutz)

Ernst Cramer was in Augsburg when the war ended. He decided to stay in Germany. (Axel Springer Unternehmensarchiv Berlin)

Joseph Eaton returned to survey the damage done to Nuremberg, his hometown. (United States Holocaust Memorial Museum, Joseph Eaton collection)

At the end of the war Samson Knoll was stationed in Marburg, where he interrogated Germans applying for licenses in media, academia, and the arts. (Art Resource)

German prisoners of war are interrogated after V-E Day for discharge and return to civilian life. Photograph by J. W. Wilton (U.S. Army Signal Corps, National Archives and Records Administration)

Hans Habe set up regional newspapers for American-occupied Germany. He is shown seated at his desk, surrounded by the MRB men he'd assigned to work with him. Left to right: #2 Ernst Wynder, #3 Konrad Kellen, #5 Stefan Heym, #6 Louis Atlas, #7 Peter Wyden, #9 Joseph Eaton. (United States Holocaust Memorial Museum, Joseph Eaton collection)

Chapter 6

The Push Into Germany

By midwinter of 1944 I had worn undershirt and pants, winter undershirt and pants, a sweater, a ski parka, olive-drab flannel pants and shirt, combat pants, a second sweater, a British leather cold-weather vest, combat jacket, scarf, wool helmet, helmet, and, finally, an overcoat. The overcoat had my mittens pinned on the sleeves like a child's, so I wouldn't lose them when tired. Sometimes people ask me now about the Battle of the Bulge, and I have to start with the clothes, and being cold and tired and having the flu. By the time I get to the bullets, they have wandered off.[306]

After the liberation of Paris, there was an organizational shift within the 2nd and the 3rd MRB companies. Captain Maxwell Grabove was relieved of his command of the 2nd MRB company and Lieutenant, later Captain, Arthur Jaffe was named as his successor. There was also a major reorganization of the companies themselves: "All of the propaganda men of the Third Company were placed on DS [double strength] with the Second Company and all of the technical radio personnel of the Second Company were placed with the Third Company."[307]

One of the 2nd MRB company's greatest triumphs came during the period when the men were still stationed in Versailles:

> A recording truck under T/Sgt [radio engineer Raymond] Wilson and a loudspeaker unit under T/Sgt [propaganda editor Peter] Weidenreich [i.e. Wyden] as announcer [...] assisted in the surrender negotiations of General-Major von Elster and 20,000 Germans in the area south of the Loire River. The ceremony between the German General and the American Major General [Robert] Macon of the 83rd Inf[antry] Div[ision] was recorded and flown to London immediately, as presumably the first that had ever been made in western Europe of a large-scale German surrender.[308]

---

[306] Arthur T. Hadley, "Is This Like Your War, Sir?"
[307] Arthur H. Jaffe, *History, 2nd Mobile Radio Company*, 42.
[308] Arthur H. Jaffe, *History, 2nd Mobile Radio Company*, 43.

The men of the 4th and 5th MRB companies arrived in Europe after the conquest of Paris, but in time for the Battle of the Bulge. The four MRB companies were now assigned to different Army units.[309] Some of the men in the 5th MRB company remained in Versailles; the rest went on to Verdun. So, too, did the Second and Third companies, setting up in old French army barracks with the 72nd Battalion. While Captain Arthur Jaffe was stationed in Verdun, five hidden Jewish Torahs were found in town, and Jaffe, who had trained as a cantor, organized a service for the Jewish troops.[310] Philip Pines remembers that as a highlight of his army service.[311]

Various smaller teams were formed in Verdun. Edward Alexander was one of a team of six—three MRB men and three British colleagues (all German refugees)—who spent the remainder of the war in Verdun, analyzing Nazi media and propaganda reports, some of which were derived from Hellschreibers[312] the Allies had captured; these reports were then used by others in the preparation of surrender leaflets, loudspeaker appeals, and radio programming.[313] Some of the "psycho boys" were called to Luxembourg for radio work. Still others were assigned to teams that were sent to join various army units at the front, often to fire leaflets across enemy lines, and to set up microphones and make loudspeaker appeals at the front. Arthur T. Hadley had this unenviable task; still, he considered himself lucky:

> I am usually off alone, going where I want to go, firing leaflets over a whole Army front, an area about two hours fast drive in length, and now and then making a loudspeaker

---

[309] "Second Company men were, for the most part, assigned to First Army, since the Third Army detachment had been constituted under Major [Louis] Huot in Normandy from Third Company personnel and the Ninth Army team made up from Fifth Company men under Major [Edward A..] Caskey. The First Army Team was [led] by Lt. [Albert H.] Salvatori, as Chief of Operations and the group infiltrated into First Army around the middle of September, about twenty strong, and remained there until after V-E Day, growing in size to about sixty officers and enlisted men." Arthur Jaffe, *History, 2nd Mobile Radio Broadcasting Company*, 43.

[310] Author interview with Arthur Jaffe, 1 Aug. 2013.

[311] Author interview with Philip Pines, 15 Aug. 2013.

[312] Hellschreibers are field teleprinters that were invented by Rudolph Hell in the 1920s and were used during the war for press, military, and diplomatic communications over land-line and radio.

[313] Correspondence with author by Edward Alexander, 28 Aug. 2013.

broadcast. The job can be dangerous but not continually so. I am more like a bomber or fighter pilot than a ground combat soldier. I have moments of extreme danger, but am safe most of the time. My life has nowhere near the hardship and continuous risk borne by each infantryman in his exposed foxhole under artillery fire and in hostile contact twenty-four hours every day.[314]

The danger was very real, even if intermittent. In December the Battle of the Bulge caught the Allied Forces off guard, and the Americans bore the brunt of the German attack. Hadley remarked, rather tersely, "Of the six of us doing roughly the same leaflet and loudspeaker work in France and later Germany, only two are killed, one wounded."[315] This was a high percentage, even for infantrymen.

The men remaining behind in Verdun were also under intense fire. Ironically, men initially trained on the site of one of the bloodiest battles of the American Civil War were now being shelled on fields that had taken the worst poundings during World War I. Clyde Shives reported:

> "Jerry" planes came over eleven times in six hours New Year's Eve keeping us in the slit trenches all night. The next morning, the company was to move to Mauzay, France, a little town some 30 miles north of Verdun. An advanced party had moved out with equipment to ready our new home for occupation. They spent a New Year's Eve few will forget. "Jerry" bombers decided to bomb the huge Prisoner of War Enclosure near our new home and in doing so, nearly picked off the advanced party.[316]

The company managed to move up to Mauzay and settle in at the 17th century Chateau de Carmois. By the time the Ardennes offensive began, "we had units with practically every fighting unit on every active sector."[317] They were so scattered, in fact, that only about twenty

---

[314] Arthur T. Hadley, *Heads or Tails*, 86-87.
[315] Arthur T. Hadley, *Heads or Tails*, 87.
[316] [Clyde Shives], "History of the Fifth," *5th Mobile Radio Broadcasting Company*.
[317] [Clyde Shives], "History of the Fifth," *5th Mobile Radio Broadcasting Company*.

men were left at headquarters, and Lieutenant Robert Asti had to travel hundreds of miles each month to pay all the men in the 5th MRB. Meanwhile, "the Chateau became the collecting point for the spoils of war. We had German cars, motorbikes, motorcycles, lugers, rifles, helmets, and from all outward appearances, the passersby might think it was a German garrison."[318]

Like so many of the soldiers, Lt. Arthur Hadley quickly came to realize that much of the soldier's good or bad fortune in war was simply a matter of "choice," "chance," or "luck." Hadley described one instance where his good fortune was a matter of "Luck and Luck Alone":

> Mid-September, a straight stretch of country road in the rolling hills of southeast Holland between Sittard and Roermond, just east of a small bend in the Maas [Meuse] River. The autumn mist keeps rising and falling, a cover through which we six officers silently walk. [...]
> I hear the sharp whistle of incoming shells and throw myself against the grassy verge without even time to make the drainage ditch. When I pick myself up after the shells explode, I see fresh white scars on the already mutilated trees lining the road. Of the five walking with me two are unhurt. One slightly wounded. Two seriously. One of these two is dying.[...]
> My jump had been no faster, farther, wiser than the others. *Luck* had decided.[319]

Captain Arthur Jaffe of the 2nd MRB company recalls an example of his own good fortune: "I was patrolling a field with (Technical Sergeant) Bert Anger and all of a sudden he threw me to the ground. I had been about to step on a land mine. Bert Anger saved my life."[320]

As a driver, Eddie Amicone of the 2nd MRB faced constant danger. During the Battle of the Bulge and the incursion into Germany, he often transported a colonel to the front lines to make loudspeaker appeals. They drove in an open Jeep with a cloth top. The Germans had timed their December 1944 counter-offensive to coincide with overcast skies that prevented the U.S. planes from providing air cover. Eddie

---

[318] [Clyde Shives], "History of the Fifth," *5th Mobile Radio Broadcasting Company.*
[319] Arthur T. Hadley, *Heads or Tails*, 89-90.
[320] Author interview with Arthur H. Jaffe, 1 Aug. 2013.

Amicone recalls, "The weather was freezing [...], and visibility was so low that American planes couldn't drop bombs. After three or four days the weather broke and American planes were able to assist in pushing the Germans back. That was the beginning of the end of the war in Germany. They were pushed all the way back to Berlin [...]." As for Amicone,

> I missed death four times. I was driving through Germany with the colonel and the Germans started shelling the road I was on with planes. The shells hit the Jeep in front of mine and killed two American soldiers. Another time, a German plane flew over our Jeep again (it was about as high as a telephone pole), close enough that we could see the pilot. We jumped out of the vehicle and hid in the woods until the plane was gone. Another time the roads were so bad from oil drips from tanks and other vehicles that my truck slid towards a ditch and my truck rolled upside down. What saved us was the gun rack mounted on the vehicle. [...] Amazingly, none of us was even injured. The colonel that I drove around ended up being killed by a German plane, though luckily I wasn't the one driving him that day. I still to this day don't know what happened to that driver, or even why I wasn't driving the colonel that day.[321]

Not all the Sharpe men were as fortunate as Amicone. Lt. Jack Collette of the 3rd MRB company was killed in action near Mainz, Germany, when he disregarded the warnings of an infantry commander and headed towards a pocket of Germans on a hog-calling mission. Charles Leveille, also of the 3rd MRB, was killed while driving a jeep out on a similar mission. Walter Straus, 2nd MRB company, son of the famous operetta composer Oscar Straus, died differently, but no less

---

[321] Letter to author from Eddie Amicone, 22 Nov. 2013. The Colonel was probably Colonel Flynn Andrew. Andrew had a reputation of being "a fool for wanting to get too far forward," although Arthur Hadley remembers him as "actually [...] a very careful and thorough soldier." Still, Hadley allowed, "He was aggressive. The loudspeaker broadcast is different from any other. It is fighting; the rest of PW [Psychological Warfare] is not." Cited in Daniel Lerner, Psychological Warfare against Nazi Germany, 249. Andrew was hit in Belgium on December 23, 1944, and died of his wounds on January 2nd.

tragically. Walter had received a medical discharge from the army after two years' service in England; in September 1945 he committed suicide in a Baltimore hotel room.

Six of the members of the 2nd MRB company received the purple heart. Bert Anger was one of these. It happened on the drive to Berlin, outside Leipzig: "I was too near an exploding mortar shell and got a few splinters in my body."[322] His friend Otto Schoeppler suffered a similar injury: "I was in the rear seat of a Jeep [...]—a cross road was under German artillery fire. I got hit by a shell fragment on the left side of my upper back."[323]

Danger loomed even for interrogators working with the German prisoners of war housed in temporary camps just behind the Allies' front lines. In one extreme case Lieutenant Albert Rosenberg, of the 4th MRB, was ordered into a German POW camp in Lorraine, near Metz, to deal with a problem that had arisen there. In this camp, as in all the German POW camps, the prisoners maintained their military ranks and discipline; this gave the prisoners an internal form of self-administration. But this camp had an unusually strong contingent of prisoners who were violently pro-Nazi. These men formed secret courts that watched the other prisoners and killed any of those who made comments critical of Hitler. "Here were captured German soldiers," Rosenberg recalls, "and among the prisoners were some who were happy that they had been captured." These men were particularly desirable subjects for Allied interrogation, but they were now in grave danger from the camp's Nazis, and American intelligence decided that it must "figure out how strong this Nazi orientation was." It was Rosenberg's assignment to masquerade as a German prisoner of war, enter the camp, and determine the names and number of Nazi thugs who were causing the killings. The entire mission must be kept secret, Rosenberg said, because, if knowledge of these camp killings became public, the Allies' entire program of encouraging peaceful German surrender would be in jeopardy, and many more American lives might be lost.[324]

Rosenberg had his own reasons for fearing the fanatical Nazis in the camp. In 1937, while a student at the University of Göttingen, he had been savagely attacked by a group of Nazi storm troopers. Before

---

[322] Bert W. Anger, "From Hanover to the Elbe," 12.
[323] Letter to author from Otto Schoeppler, 2 Sept. 2013.
[324] Author interview with Albert Rosenberg, 13 Jan. 2014.

some non-Jewish friends could rescue him, he had suffered a broken jaw and severe spinal damage. Now he was entering an enclosure of prisoners that was known to harbor Nazi murderers.

All aspects of his mission were "painstakingly prepared." He should have "nothing to worry about." He dressed in the uniform of a captured SS soldier and entered the camp with a body of new prisoners. Once in the camp, he circulated among the other prisoners, sounding them out for information about the camp's internal operations. The Nazis quickly grew suspicious, and Rosenberg tried to make his way over to the chain-link fence that surrounded the camp and reach an American guard. "Everyone was watching everybody else," he remembered. "I was trying to get out," but the situation "had become dangerous." Before he could reach a guard, Rosenberg was surrounded by Nazi killers. Even seventy years after the fact, Rosenberg breaks into a sweat when he tells his story. Finally, he was able to call to a guard, "I am an American officer! Get me out! Now!" Fortunately, larger numbers of GIs came to his rescue and he got out of the camp unharmed.[325]

It would not be until after the Battle of the Bulge that the armored "talking tank" was used for making broadcasts directly into enemy lines. A Russian emigrant, an OSS civilian named Alexis Sammaripa—the only civilian ever to command a U.S. tank during the war—was the first to mount a loudspeaker on a Third Armored Division tank. Unfortunately, not even the tank provided him with sufficient protection. In March 1945 he was killed while appealing to the Germans to surrender.

At the same time that Sammaripa was using his tank for propaganda purposes, Arthur Hadley finally succeeded in persuading his superiors to allow him to use a light M5A1 tank of the Second Armored Division for a similar purpose. It was, he noted, a difficult proposition: "I was a young lieutenant in the position of having to persuade a tank general to give up a fighting vehicle for a loudspeaker." Finally, Hadley was able to persuade the general that by getting his loudspeakers off the ground and mounted on tanks, they "would be mobile and infinitely more effective during an attack." Hadley described how it worked:

> At last, we could broadcast our message during an attack.

---

[325] Author interview with Albert Rosenberg, 13 Jan. 2014.

This was an advantage because the enemy was more likely to surrender during an attack than after the battle had quieted down.

The jury-rigged tank also worked remarkably well. The loudspeaker itself was mounted on the forward slope of the turret and partly covered by a metal casing that resisted light machine-gun fire. The generator was set over the engine in the rear, totally covered. All the tank's weapons could operate, though the wires attached to the speaker limited turret motion. Some of the ammunition racks inside the tank were removed and the amplifiers for the loudspeaker fastened to the steel insides.

We broadcasters lived in the turret, the tank driver was forward in the driver's compartment and the electrician who maintained the loudspeaker and electronic equipment occupied the assistant driver's seat.

Hadley's qualifications for broadcasting from this "Talking Tank" were rather unique: "Having trained as a tanker, I was familiar with tank combat. I could work the radios and fire the guns. I usually placed the tank as No. 3 in an attack column. There, it could broadcast immediately without interfering with the two point tanks as they checked right and left."[326]

Hadley described one tank mission that ran like clockwork:

> The tank mounted loudspeaker was operating with an advance column of the 2d Armored Division. Arriving before a fortified town the column deployed. Some fire was received from the town. The loudspeaking tank informed the garrison of the town that a large armored task force stood on the outskirts. The broadcast also informed the people that the commander didn't want to destroy the town. The garrison was then informed that American artillery was ranged on them.
>
> Over the tank communications system, word was sent back to the artillery. Six leaflet shells, containing surrender instructions for towns, burst over the village. The occupants of the town were then informed that American fighter-bombers were overhead. The Forward Air Controller called down a P-

---

[326] Arthur T. Hadley, "Firing Potent Words, From a Tank," *New York Times*, 25 Sept. 2006.

47, that laid a leaflet bomb squarely over the center of the town. The tanks then moved forward without firing, while the loudspeaker continued to call on the town to surrender. As the tanks brushed through a light curtain of fire, the firing stopped and white flags appeared. A garrison of some 800 men with anti-tank weapons surrendered.[327]

Later in the war, Arthur Hadley's luck ran out. He was ambushed by a wire stretched across the road, which knocked him from his Jeep. "I remember flying through the air toward a great, dull, red void. Then just black."[328] When he came to, he managed to make it to his overturned Jeep and tap out an SOS on the horn. His wound proved serious. Three operations in France failed to mend his leg, and it was only after his return to the States that a surgeon was able to repair it.

It was the leaflet and loudspeaker men, and the drivers and technicians, who experienced the worst of the fighting. As part of a leaflet and loudspeaker team operating on the Siegfried line, Captain Gaston Pender experienced both the danger of facing down desperate, cornered German troops and the exhilaration of calling in great numbers of surrendering soldiers. Pender sent his wife a report of the conflict around Geilenkirchen, a small town located near the border with the Netherlands, about twelve miles north of Aachen:

> The night before, we fired leaflets to the Germans. Then about 10 a.m. we made our first broadcast. We were about 1,000 yards from the town. I put the loudspeaker on top of a bunker of the Siegfried line and Sergeant Rapoport talked from inside the pillbox. The prisoners began coming in very slowly. At 11:30 we broadcast again from another spot on the Siegfried line which was just outside Geilenkirchen. A few more prisoners wandered in. Our troops then entered the town. I stayed with my crew behind the railroad just before the town. After the first platoon had entered the town I moved up with my boys to the first row of houses, which were behind another railroad. Plenty of rifle fire and machine gun fire popping away, and prisoners coming in in groups.

---

[327] Arthur T. Hadley, "The 'Propaganda' Tank," in William E. Daugherty, *A Psychological Warfare Casebook*, 567.
[328] Arthur T. Hadley, *Heads or Tails*, 97.

Lieutenant Preston and I crawled to the top of a bomb-wrecked rail over-pass and put the loudspeaker in amidst the twisted iron. We wanted to talk to a few prisoners to get more information before we went on the air for the third time. The prisoners which had been taken were being assembled and guarded behind a warehouse which was some 100 yards from where the press and I were hiding. The Americans started to march the prisoners toward us, and as they did so, a German machine gun opened up from about 200 yards further up and killed one of their own men and wounded two more. None of our boys were hit. [...]

Then we went into the middle of town and went into a house which was supposed to have some Germans left in it. About that time Sergeant Rapoport opened up with the loudspeaker and 47 prisoners walked out of the house with their hands up. Ninety per cent of them were carrying our leaflets and were only waiting for us to arrive for them to surrender. I got a jeep full of German sub-machine guns and other things. [...]

We started back toward the jeep walking along the road. A sniper opened up on us—and we hit the dirt again. I shall never forget the whine of those bullets.

Pender, like Hadley, felt that the danger he faced was minor compared with that faced every hour of every day by those who served in the infantry: "Those men should get a lot of credit. They are the boys who do the dirty work."[329]

The men in military intelligence at least got some time off. Gunter Kosse remembers living with his IPW team in a basement in Hürtgen, where, despite the heavy fighting, they had a stove, and could play solitaire or read the *Reader's Digest* in their downtime.[330] On Christmas Eve, they ventured out through the village to look for some coal for their stove. They found some lying on a board in a shed behind one of the houses and, when they raised the board, they also found lots of

---

[329] "Former Local Officer Tells of War Action," *The Gettysburg Times*, 19 Feb. 1945.
[330] Located on the German-Belgian border, the town had been taken by the Americans on November 29th, 1944 during the second phase of the Battle of the Hürtgen Forest. The battle itself continued until December 16th.

Christmas tree ornaments—glass balls, tinsel, and such. They broke through a plaster wall into another room of the shed; there they found two chests containing beautiful chinaware and table linens. They cut down a tree in the woods, decorated it, and celebrated their own little "Christmas miracle" in their basement shelter.[331]

After Christmas, Kosse's IPW team was kept busy trying to extract information from dozens of German prisoners each week. He and the other members of his team received a commendation noting their superior performance, and all received a promotion.[332] Kosse believes that much of his team's success stemmed from the fact that its members all came from different parts of the German Reich: he was from Berlin, for example, Bert Steinberg was from Frankfurt, and Herbert Klein was from Vienna. Five of the six men on the team were Jewish. Kosse recalls that no two interrogations were alike. During one particularly unusual interrogation, Bert Steinberg discovered that the older Volkssturm prisoner they were questioning had been a cutter at his father's cloth manufacturing business in Frankfurt. Since this man was clearly anti-Nazi and fighting under duress, the team members sent him further behind the Allied lines with a bottle of whiskey, two cartons of cigarettes, and chocolate, along with a letter recommending him for leniency.[333]

Lt. Albert Rosenberg's team[334] is another that was cited for its effectiveness. It, too, reflected a wide spread of linguistic ability:

> Every member of the team either was born in the German-speaking area of Europe or was brought there at a comparatively early age. Every member had received higher education, some part (if not all) of it in Germany. Every member was at least bilingual, most were trilingual, and several quadrilingual. Their pooled resources comprised some familiarity with all the major European languages, including the Scandinavian. More

---

[331] Author interview with Gunter Kosse, 9 Oct. 2013.
[332] Kosse was promoted from Private to T/5; as officer in charge of the team, Lt. Roland G. Woller was promoted to Captain. The team was then attached to the Third Army Interrogation Center. (Information from Dan Gross.)
[333] Author interview with Gunter Kosse, 9 Oct. 2013.
[334] Known as the "Kampfgruppe Rosenberg," the team included Richard Akselrad, Ernest Biberfeld, Leo Fialkoff, Michael Josselson, Max Kimenthal, and Alfred Sampson.

important, among them they had some mastery of every important dialect of the German language as actually spoken in Germany and Austria.[335]

These men, too, had to work with each prisoner on an individual basis:

> In "processing" so large and incessant a flow [of German prisoners], they had perforce to operate by "feel" (as some of them put it, by "smell") in rapidly separating strong Nazis from non-Nazis, lies from truthful responses, voluble from tongue-tied personalities.[336]

The MRB radio men were on the move during this time. Phil Pines of the 2nd MRB had been summoned to Verdun, where he, Henry Longley, and Olcott Dole were assigned to the command of Lieutenant Louis Muhlbauer and sent to the 9th Army to set up a broadcasting unit for war correspondents in Maastricht, Holland; this was the first Dutch city to have been liberated by the Allied forces. They passed through Liège[337] as buzz bombs exploded all around them, found that the bridge across the Meuse River had been bombed, and only with some difficulty were able to find and cross another bridge to get to Maastricht. From there they moved to Bemelen, where the transmitter was located on a hill three miles east of Maastricht. They now broadcast under the call letters JEEP (Jig Easy Easy Peter), since the First Army station, JESQ, had gone out of operation after the Germans took over Spa, Belgium. Pines recalls:

> Our transmission signals were like honey to bees in attracting German planes. On January 1, 1945, they were extremely active near us. Our antiaircraft cannons shot down one of them that crashed about 100 feet from our unit.
>
> Dole, the driver of our 3/4 ton truck, insisted on picking up our lieutenant in Maastricht at the regular time. Normally, he went alone. I went with him this time. We were chased by a German plane and raced to a wooded area, pulled to the side, and dived into a ditch. When the plane left, we resumed our

---

[335] Daniel Lerner, *Psychological Warfare against Nazi Germany*, 77.
[336] Daniel Lerner, *Psychological Warfare against Nazi Germany*, 77-8.
[337] Until September 1946 Liège was written "Liége."

trip. As we were crossing the Queen Wilhelmina Bridge, another German plane dived at us. We raced across, picked up the lieutenant, and brought him to our unit. [...]

[This] was the first time we had trouble from German planes. The reason was that we had no air support. Our airfields were out of operation, because they were fog bound.[338]

Pines broadcast a number of well-known correspondents at Bemelen, among them Howard K. Smith and William Randall "Bill" Downs (two of Edward R. Murrow's "boys" with CBS) and BBC war correspondents Robert Barr, Chester Wilmott, and Stanley Maxted.

From Maastricht, Lieutenant Muhlbauer's team accompanied the troops of the 9th army, crossing the Rhine on infantry landing barges that had been used at Normandy. As they moved through Germany, they found destruction everywhere. Much of the bombing appeared arbitrary. As they passed through the industrial city of Duisburg, Phil Pines was surprised to see that the homes were all destroyed, but the huge Thyssen Steelworks were untouched: "It seemed to me it should have been the other way around."[339] The 9th Army was able to advance forty miles a day, through Hameln, through Helmstedt, where they crossed the big bridge the day before it was destroyed by the Germans, and on to Klein Wanzleben, near the Elbe. On their way, they spent a night at Joseph Goebbels's old home estate; the men slept in the guards' building, while the officers slept in the actual estate house. And at Klein Wanzleben they put up their tents "on the grounds of the man who had been in charge of all slave labor in Germany, while the officers stayed in his big mansion."[340]

Bert Anger also made it to the Elbe. Here, on April 25th, the American forces met up with the Russian army:

---

[338] Letter to author from Philip Pines, 22 October 2013.
[339] Author interview with Philip Pines, 15. Aug. 2013. The British had changed their bombing strategies after discovering that the Germans could quickly rebuild factories; it was far more effective—and demoralizing—to bomb the areas of town where the factory workers were housed. See Alan J. Levine, *The Strategic Bombing of Germany, 1940–1945*, 36.
[340] Author interview with Philip Pines, 15. Aug. 2013. Pines is probably alluding to Fritz Sauckel, General Commissioner for Labor Deployment from 1942 until the end of the war. I have found no mention of an estate in Klein Wanzleben.

There were no civilians left in the city called Torgau. There were many Russians on the shore, but no Americans were allowed to cross to the Russian side of the river. There was much toasting with yellowish vodka that the Russians brought, and drinking out of a broken cup and saluting Roosevelt, Churchill, and Stalin. My World War II experience ended with a terrible migraine headache the next morning.[341]

Whether it was interrogation, appeal by loudspeaker, pamphlet, or radio, the services of the MRB men had been strained to the limits in the final push through Germany. Even the irrepressible gossip columnist Igor Cassini became something of a war hero in these last days of the war, although unintentionally. Like many of the Sharpe soldiers, he coveted a German Luger—a semi-automatic pistol that, for its time, was state of the art. Cassini had, by this time, transferred out of his MRB unit and joined *Stars and Stripes*, the U.S. army newspaper, where he was assigned as a writer for *Warweek*, the magazine section of the paper. He and seven others rotated assignments to the front. Cassini was told to cover the battle for Nuremberg (Nürnberg). He filed his story, then decided to find the Luger that he craved:

> Nuremberg is laced with underground passages and catacombs. I saw a cave and walked into it, figuring it might be a logical place for the Nazis to cache weapons.
> It was dark inside, and I turned on my flashlight. That is when I came face to face with a German officer. Before I could grab my carbine or panic, he offered me his gun, and asked in excellent English, "May I surrender, sir?"
> I accepted the surrender (with a sigh of relief): 1,200 men along with 2,000 civilians. I signaled to the nearby troops. A corporal came over with reinforcements to round them up.[342]

To Cassini's dismay, this American corporal shot and killed one unfortunate old man, who did not move out quickly enough, but stooped, instead, to pick up something he had dropped. "For a split second," Cassini commented, "I hated to be an American, as if a German, in the corporal's place would have been more humane. [...] I do not know why I remember it or why it affected me so." Seeing that he

---

[341] Bert W. Anger, "From Hanover to the Elbe," 12-13.
[342] Igor Cassini, *I'd do it all over again*, 101.

could do nothing, Cassini set off "on a glorious spree, one of the forms of sanity for which I have a gift. Despite the confusion of capturing 3,200 Germans by mistake, I managed to get my Luger, and by the time I reported back to Paris, I also had two cars, three motorcycles, two typewriters, two French girls, and a liberated Italian prisoner of war, Antonio, who became my valet for a month."[343]

At the end of the war, Cassini left the Army with an honorable discharge and three battle stars.[344] As for the other Sharpe soldiers: "All of the field detachments were called in and dissolved with the personnel being given new tasks in the information control phase of the occupation." The war was over, but the battle for German hearts and minds was to be continued, under military governance.

---

[343] Igor Cassini, *I'd do it all over again*, 102.
[344] Igor Cassini, *I'd do it all over again*, 108.

Chapter 7

Confronting the Camps

> *How many poets and painters have there been who did pass through Hell, not some imaginary Hell, but the real Hell of war and Holocaust? Not many, and fewer ever survive. Those who do may therefore have a special obsession—to bear witness. They can never escape from what they witnessed or resist describing what they saw, indescribable as it is.*[345]

The MRB men had not been forewarned about the horrors of the Nazi concentration camps, in part because of the fear the Allied leaders had that, by calling attention to the camps, there might be bad public fall-out by making the war appear to be a "Jewish" one, and in part for fear that, if the recent émigrés were told of these atrocities, they might prove less focused on their immediate task at hand. Many of the Sharpe soldiers had families in Europe, and many of these families were Jews. And, in truth, even the top army brass was unaware of the extent of the atrocities that had occurred in these camps. At least two of the Camp Sharpe men—Ernst Cramer and Henry Deku (Heinz Dekuczynski) of the 2nd MRB company—had been imprisoned in Buchenwald before being allowed to leave Germany. Entering the camps, then, was even more horrifying for the foreign-born MRB men than it was for many of the native American GIs—they had family members, friends, and neighbors who might be among the emaciated survivors of the camps, or, more likely, among their victims.

But even the most battle-hardened soldiers who entered the gates of camps such as Buchenwald, Bergen Belsen, and Dachau were horrified by the inhumanity they saw there. In early April, American-born 5th MRB member Arthur Hadley came upon his first camp near Magdeburg, Germany:

> We turn a sharp corner and before us are barbed wire walls. I'm alert expecting to be fired at. The two tanks ahead of me traverse their guns. Then I see dead bodies, all withered

---

[345] Si Lewen, *Reflections and Repercussions: A Memoir*, Chapter 18.

hanging on the wire. I am amazed that men could be so barbarous as to string up corpses. Then some of the corpses on the barbed wire move. A few actually half wave. Not with their arms, just wiggle and flop their wrists. I am not looking at the dead but at the starved living. Every horror I had seen or imagined fell short of this reality. [...] Since then, I reject as totally false any belief that mankind are born good.

Because German tanks were going into position on the far side of the ridge, Hadley's unit could not stop; the men could only pause long enough to loosen their ration crates from their tanks and throw the cases off for these prisoners. As they left, Hadley saw men "crawling, not walking, crawling toward the food. I wonder how they will get the cases open."[346]

Samson Knoll entered Buchenwald with the American liberating forces and took photographs of the camp and some of its emaciated survivors. Ernst Cramer also entered with the American liberators: "It was terrible seeing the concentration camp again. What I found was much more horrible than anything I had experienced myself, seven years before."[347] He found corpses "piled like wood, and people were dying in front of us," in part because the U.S. Army rations were too rich for their bodies to tolerate.[348] The colonel sitting next to him on the drive back from the camp commented, "Ernie, after seeing that, I can understand that you don't want to have anything more to do with Germany." Cramer answered, "Colonel, I have to surprise you. Today I have decided to accept your offer to work in the military government."[349]

Albert Rosenberg entered Buchenwald on April 16th. In addition to viewing the regular camp, he went to *Das kleine Lager*, the notorious "Small Camp," where evacuees from Auschwitz and Birkenau were housed. Here the conditions were considerably worse than in the main camp. These prisoners had no food, no water, and no shelter, just a couple of windowless, doorless barracks. Rosenberg felt that the pris-

---

[346] Arthur T. Hadley, *Heads or Tails*, 95.
[347] "Ich will nicht verdrängen!" *Bild*, 28 Jan. 2013. All translations from this article are my own.
[348] "Around the Jewish World: Germany's Past and Future Reflected in Honor for German Jewish Journalist," *JTA, The Global Jewish News Source*, 17 Oct. 2003.
[349] "Ich will nicht verdrängen!" *Bild*, 28 Jan. 2013.

oners there, Jews from many different countries, were "not human" anymore. Nor had anyone been able to make them realize that they had been liberated. Rosenberg cut out a large cardboard Jewish star, which he attached to his uniform, cleared a space, and addressed the prisoners in Yiddish, explaining to them that the Americans had come to help them. In addition, he asked for information from those few prisoners still able to speak to him.[350]

Rosenberg repressed the memory of what he found in this camp for many years. After the memory came back to him, the horror returned to him each night. "The stenches keep coming back," he remarked, "the recurring stench of Buchenwald."[351] Rosenberg's driver, a non-Jewish army sergeant, died in an automobile accident soon after the visit to *Das kleine Lager*; Rosenberg is convinced that his death was a suicide, brought on by the horrors that he witnessed there.

Si Lewen had already seen a number of Nazi work camps, and he delayed going to Buchenwald, out of fear, perhaps, that he might find some of his old Berlin friends there. When he finally did go, a couple of weeks after the camp's liberation, it was a horrifying experience for him:

> A foul stench still hung in the air and in the eyes of the recently condemned who still occupied the same old barracks. Its inmates continued to be contained within the same camp long after its liberation; "D.P." (Displaced Persons) camps had not yet been organized. More and more inmates began to surround me as I tried to make my way around the camp. They looked more like recently bald skeletons than alive, even though now on a diet of "G.I." rations. Some tried to smile; it seemed more a grotesque grimace; but they had survived. "How long will we have to remain here? When can we leave? Can we come to America?" were some of the questions. "I'll see what I can do," I lied. They followed wherever I tried to go, repeating the same questioning stares. I tried to avoid them, especially their eyes which all appeared overly large within their emaciated faces. [...] They appeared unrecognizable, almost non-human.[352]

For Lewen, the encounters in this camp proved to be his breaking

---

[350] Albert Rosenberg interview with Sylvia Cohen, Tape 4.
[351] Albert Rosenberg interview with Sylvia Cohen, Tape 5.
[352] Si Lewen, *Reflections and Repercussions*, Chapter 18.

point:

> Trying to avoid the horror I saw in their faces, I pulled away, again and again, and finally succeeded to elude the group which had followed me about. Eventually, I found myself alone, in Buchenwald's crematorium. Its ovens were cool now, the oven doors wide open but still begrimed with the soot and ashes of its recently cremated. I turned away into the darkest corner and sank to my knees and baring my head I prayed and broke down and cried, but quickly gathered myself as I heard some people entering, and bolted past them and out—"out, out, out, out, out!"
>
> Soon after, I checked into the nearest medical station: I was urinating and vomiting blood worse than ever and my insides felt like one wrenching mess. I knew that I was finished as a soldier, seeing the world for what, I thought, it was: a slaughterhouse, a bordello and an insane asylum, run by butchers, pimps and madmen. [...] A hospital ship brought me back to America and half a year later I was discharged—"as good as new" one of the doctors said. I was not so sure.[353]

After the war, Lewen would immortalize the horror of this visit to Buchenwald in a haunting narrative sequence of 72 black and white images on paper called *A Journey* (1958-1963).

The Americans had entered Buchenwald on April 11, 1945. A week later the Buchenwald subcamp at Thekla, a suburb of Leipzig and only a five-minute ride from the Leipzig train station, became the setting for an even more deliberate atrocity. Bert Anger and Otto Schoeppler first arrived just two hours after this atrocity occurred; a few days later, Schoeppler wrote up the report for his superiors, based on what he was told by two of the survivors. It read, in part:

> Many of the political prisoners at Thekla arrived only within the last month, they were evacuated westward to avoid having them fall into Russian hands. There were some 650 prisoners who started this evacuation trip. They went by foot [...;] as this forced march progressed many of them grew too

---

[353] Si Lewen, *Reflections and Repercussions: A Memoir*, Chapter 18.

weak to go on. Those who fell by the wayside were stripped and then shot by the guards, the other prisoners had to bury them were they fell. Thus the march continued. One man knew of 166 such graves along the way. [...]

Then came the time when Leipzig was threatened by the rapidly advancing American troops. Something had to be done with these prisoners [...]. The healthiest of the prisoners were taken out, these men appeared to be physically capable of doing some more forced labor for their murderous masters. These men were last seen walking eastward in the direction of [the town of] TAUCHA. This left some 325 political prisoners behind, and American spearheads were drawing closer. The SS guards were showing more signs of nervousness. Then it happened, it was the 18 of April, one PM, only one hour before the American spearheads entered LEIPZIG. This was the hour which meant a flaming inferno of hell to these 325 political prisoners, instead of liberation from the horrible life they had been subjected to.

It was at one PM on the 18 of April that the SS guards ordered these 325 people into one barrack, gave the order to close all doors and windows and put up all blackouts. This was done. There were 325 defenseless persons in one small building, all doors and windows closed and all blackouts in place. The next step began one of the most atrocious massacres ever recorded. The SS guards stood around this barrack and turned it into a mass of flame by firing incendiary grenades into it. The barrack was turned into a screaming burning mass of human beings. Then even a German tank lumbered up and fired a round into the building. The persons trapped in this flaming inferno, hurled themselves at doors and windows in an effort to escape, this was met by a hail of small arms fire, as well as machine gun fire from the tank. Those who did break out were shot and were left where they fell, their clothes still burning. Some got as far as the concertina wire, here they were either shot or burned to death, their charred bodies are still entangled in this wire. Others managed to get beyond all of the barbed wire barriers but were killed in the open field surrounding the enclosure. The most amazing thing of all is that some of these people did manage to escape with their lives. The exact number is not known, but it varies from 4 to 50. Probably the only reason they managed to escape was because the guards responsible for the massacre fled after the first few minutes for fear they might yet be captured. One of the persons escaped by climbing down into an outdoor latrine, 2 others hid in a locomotive boiler for 2 days before they dared come out.

These people lived to tell this story. Yet this story, unbelievable as it may sound, is told in still another way. It is written in the blood and ashes of those who had their lived taken at this ruthless massacre of THEKLA.[354]

Schoeppler had already seen Buchenwald. "Buchenwald was horrible," he noted, "Thekla was savage."[355]

While Schoeppler wrote up his report of the Thekla massacre, Bert Anger took photographs of the carnage. He, like most soldiers, had thought that the rumors he had heard of mass murders were merely propaganda, like that propagated during the First World War, when the German soldiers "were supposed to have murdered and eaten Belgian children." Now, however, he saw that these rumors were all true:

> It was a sight I will never forget. Never! I took a lot of photographs that day, drove back to Leipzig and went into a drugstore and told the druggist that he should develop the film. And that if anything happened to the film, I would personally shoot him. And I would certainly have done that. But the man gave the film back to me the next day, with tears in his eyes, and said he simply could not believe that something like that was possible.[356]

At the camps some of the MRB men not only had to confront the horrors that had been perpetrated upon people whom they might have known and loved, but the fact that they, as Germans, shared the same genetic makeup as the monsters who had committed those crimes. They were put in the difficult position of being forced to identify not only with the victims of the camps but also with the men who had served as its guards and murderers. This was part of the nightmare vi-

---

[354] Otto Schoeppler, Confidential report entitled "Political concentration camp THEKLA." I have corrected the few typographical errors in this report.

[355] Letter from Otto Schoeppler to author, 18 Aug. 2013.

[356] Cited in Christian Bauer, Rebekka Göpfert, *Die Ritchie Boys*, 169-170. All translations from this volume are my own.

sion that Si Lewen portrayed in his graphic series "A Journey," and one that disturbed many of the men from Camp Sharpe. They themselves were Germans. How was it possible for people like themselves to allow such horrors to occur?

In speaking with the defeated Germans, the MRB men heard, again and again, the justification that they had had no wish to cause evil. They had not known of the horrors of the camps and, besides, what could they, the "little people" have done? Stefan Heym asked himself, "Did he really have to tell himself, in the light of these cowardly wretches, *There, but for the Grace of God, go I?*"[357] His answer was a resounding "No, no, no.":

> Those who had followed the brown-shirted Pied Piper had really done it because he showed them the more comfortable path, and because it was more fun to march along, side by side and in sync with the boots of power, than it was to pause and to ask oneself where this path would lead. And how pleasant it had been, not just to obey, but also, now and then, to be able to give commands, to have a grain of this great power in their own hands! [358]

Ernst Cramer saw the Holocaust as a tragedy for both Jewish and non-Jewish Germans:

> The breach with civilization that the Nazis carried out, and in which many Germans collaborated in so many ways, was the greatest disaster in German history. Never before had Germany sunk so far. Without confusing between victims and perpetrators, or equating them at all, it can be said: The greatest affliction in the history of the Jews was, at the same time—like two sides of destiny's mirror—the greatest disaster in the history of the Germans.
>
> I know what I am talking about for, as a German Jew, I belong to both groups.[359]

Stefan Heym, Ernst Cramer, and most of the other MRB men who

---

[357] Stefan Heym, *Nachruf*, 363.
[358] Stefan Heym, *Nachruf*, 363-364.
[359] Ernst Cramer, "Worst Disaster in German History. Have we learned the lesson of Auschwitz?"

had grown up on the European continent, came to believe that the Germans could be saved only by a national program of reeducation: "Education is required. [...] We can best honor the victims of the National Socialist tyranny by seeing to it with all means at our disposal that nothing like it ever happens again—or, more realistically, by making sure that nothing like that can happen again on German or, indeed, on European soil."[360]

At first the American military government appeared to agree with the MRB men. After visiting the camp with Generals Patton and Bradley, General Eisenhower decided that Buchenwald should be seen by as many people as possible before its liberated prisoners were sent back to their homes. Journalists and newscasters from around the world were invited to Buchenwald to see the dimensions of the barbarity for themselves and to report on what had happened there. Margaret Bourke-White did a photo essay on Buchenwald for *Life Magazine*. American congressmen and British parliamentarians visited the camp. And General Eisenhower ordered Albert Rosenberg to give a tour of Buchenwald to the citizens of Weimar, in order that they face their own complicity in the horrors that had occurred there. Many of these citizens wept as they looked upon the emaciated prisoners and exhibits showing the methods of punishment and execution that had been practiced there. The German reaction was like that of the druggist in Leipzig, "I didn't know."[361]

The MRB men, many of whom had experienced hateful persecution in Germany themselves, did not accept this attempt at self-justification. They had seen for themselves how Germans had simply looked away when they saw hooligans brutalizing those who had once been their friends and neighbors. Some, like Albert Rosenberg and Curt Jellin, had experienced this violence personally; they had been savagely beaten by Nazi thugs while they were still living in pre-war Germany. Albert Rosenberg remarked:

> SHAEF was very smart to give me the job of tour guide that day. They couldn't have gotten anyone better. Those people claimed to be innocent, but I knew they weren't. I knew that because I knew them. They said they were crying because

---

[360] Ernst Cramer, "Worst Disaster in German History. Have we learned the lesson of Auschwitz?"

[361] "The liberation of Buchenwald at 3:15 p.m. on April 11, 1945."

they didn't know. But that was a lie. They were crying because they *did* know. They were hoping their tears would absolve them, as if someone would pat them on the head and say, don't worry, it's going to be all right. But they had the wrong guy for that. The trains ran to Buchenwald every day. People from Weimar worked at the Gustloff factory next to the camp. Guards lived in the town. So don't say you didn't know, because you did. *You knew.*[362]

One of the prisoners in the camp, a young Spanish communist and philosophy student named Jorge Semprún,[363] retained strong memories of Rosenberg's tour to Weimar citizens—women "wearing spring dresses in bright colors," adolescents, and old men—and his speaking to them "in a neutral, implacable voice": "'Your pretty town,' he told them, 'so clean, so neat, brimming with cultural memories, the heart of classical and enlightened Germany, seems not to have had the slightest qualm about living in the smoke of the Nazi crematoria!'"[364]

Semprún followed Rosenberg on his entire tour of Buchenwald. It lasted over two hours. "The women (a good number of them at least) were unable to restrain their tears," he recalled. They "begged for forgiveness with theatrical gestures. Some of them obligingly went so far as to feel quite faint." Meanwhile, "The adolescents took refuge in despairing silence. The old men looked away, clearly unwilling to listen to any of this."[365]

Concerned that people would forget, or deny, the atrocities committed in the German camps, General Eisenhower ordered Rosenberg to compile a detailed report about Buchenwald, one that would tell how the camp had come about, how it had been administered, and how it had functioned internally.

Rosenberg interviewed Jorge Semprún, as one of the informants who could assist in understanding Buchenwald. Semprún would always remember the hours that he spent together with this twenty-six year old soldier: "He had become an American to bear arms, to make war on Nazism. To make war on his own country, to put it bluntly. By

---

[362] Cited in Mark Jacobson, *The Lampshade*, 164.

[363] Today Semprún (1923-2011) is remembered as a screen writer and politician, who, even in his memoirs, introduced fictional scenes in an attempt to portray the "real" truth of his experience.

[364] Jorge Semprún, *Literature or Life*, 80.

[365] Jorge Semprún, *Literature or Life*, 80.

becoming an American, he had chosen the universality of the democratic cause, an abstraction that could not become reality until his country had been defeated." The two men quickly discovered a shared love for poetry and philosophy. On Semprún's name day, Rosenberg took the young prisoner on an outing to Goethe's town residence and country home, and they talked about Kant, Heidegger, Adorno, Horkheimer, and Marcuse, about Hannah Arendt, Bertolt Brecht, and Hermann Broch. Although he would never see Rosenberg again after his departure from the camp, Semprún would always retain a fond memory of this young man, with "his thin, gangling body, his sad and piercing gaze, his vast erudition,"[366] as the man who awakened in him a renewed interest in the outside world, and in learning.

Rosenberg assigned a team of ten former prisoners, representatives of different countries, political tendencies, and religious convictions, to work on his *Buchenwald Report*. He placed the writing of the main report in the hands of Eugen Kogon. His choice of Kogon was a wise one. Buchenwald was located in what would become the Russian zone, and half the camp had been run by its Communist inmates while it was under German control.[367] Eugen Kogon, however, was both a devout Catholic and an early vocal opponent of Hitler. Rosenberg speculates that, after the Russian takeover of Buchenwald, Kogon might well "have wound up in Siberia," had he not been given this privileged assignment for the U.S. military forces.[368] Instead, Kogon would go on to become a dominant voice in West German politics, by helping to establish the Christian Democratic Union (CDU) party, and by serving as international president of the European Union.[369]

---

[366] Jorge Semprún, *Literature or Life*, 97.

[367] The German Democratic Republic, which existed from 1949 to 1990, made Buchenwald a shrine to Communist resistance, noting, quite correctly, that, on April 11th, 1945, communist prisoners of the camp had "self-liberated" Buchenwald. These prisoners had had positions of power in the camp as Kapos, or camp supervisors. Some of the Kapos were fair in matters of food distribution and the life and death decisions they were called to make over their fellow prisoners; others, including a criminal element (they wore green triangles in contrast to the red triangles of the political prisoners) were not. Often, Rosenberg learned, the destruction of so many human beings in the camp was a case of prisoner against prisoner. Cf. Albert Rosenberg interview with Sylvia Cohen, Tape 5.

[368] Author interview with Albert Rosenberg, 6 Jan. 2014.

[369] Much of this information comes from David A. Hackett's Introduction to his edited and translated edition of *The Buchenwald Report*.

And Kogon already had excellent credentials. He had written his doctoral dissertation on "Fascism and Corporate State" and been pre-war editor of a prominent Catholic journal. During his nearly seven years of confinement in Buchenwald, he had acquired influence in the camp by working as clerk to Erwin Ding-Schuler, the camp doctor who headed a typhus experimentation ward; by gaining the doctor's trust, he had been able to save a number of prisoners—including three Allied flyers—by exchanging their identities with those of prisoners who had died of typhus. In addition, Kogon's socialist leanings were a plus with the camp communists, who had established their own internal system of tyranny in Buchenwald through their service as Kapos, or camp supervisors.

Rosenberg had the motivation to prepare the most thorough report possible, since he had lost twenty-eight members of his family to the Nazi Holocaust. He and part of his MRB team (Max Kimenthal, Alfred Sampson, Richard Akselrad, and Ernest Biberfeld) had come to Weimar from Frankfurt, where they had been rigorously interrogating captured Nazi prisoners. Rosenberg spent over a month in Weimar, and remained "very much involved in all phases" of the Buchenwald project.

Sometimes atrocities came to light in a very odd way. Rosenberg recalls that he was sitting at a desk one day, working up a report, "when a French prisoner came and started shouting at me, saying I was no better than the Germans. That I had no shame. Didn't I know the light I was using to write my reports had a lampshade made of human skin? [...] I found another place to do my work."[370]

Rosenberg had a SHAEF pass that allowed him a great deal of freedom. Issued in February 1945, this pass stated that "The bearer of this card will not be interfered with in the performance of his duty by the military police or any other military organization by command of General Eisenhower."[371] Rosenberg made ample use of this pass at Buchenwald. When Kogon complained to him that his team was underfed and overcrowded in the camp administrative office that had been assigned to it, Rosenberg requisitioned the Weimar home of Baldur von Schirach, the former head of the Hitler Youth and Gauleiter of Vienna, as working space for Kogon's team; he also used his SHAEF pass to requisition food for them from army headquarters at a time when food was hard to come by. In this fashion, the men working on

---

[370] Cited in Mark Jacobson, *The Lampshade*, 156.
[371] Cited in Mark Jacobson, *The Lampshade*, 164-165.

the Buchenwald report were treated to dinners of steak and shrimp, "food that ordinarily only colonels eat." By flashing his pass, Rosenberg was able to buy Kogon a home in Weimar with army funds and to bring Kogon's wife and children from Vienna to join him there.[372]

The Buchenwald Report was composed between April 16 and May 11, 1945. Besides the main text of the report, of which Kogon was the principal author, it includes 169 reports written in collaboration with 104 prisoners. It is, therefore, a unique document in that it is a collaborative project of prisoners and was composed while they were still living at the camp.

Another attempt to preserve a record of the camps came about when Colonel Clifford Powell, in his capacity as Publicity and Propaganda Warfare Officer, invited Hanuš Burger to make a film about them. He could, he was told, write the script himself, and then, once it had been approved by the Americans, send it to the English, French, and Russians for their go-ahead. At first Burger was hesitant, because he anticipated squabbles among the Allied officers. But then he thought: "Maybe somewhere up among the higher powers they were actually serious about de-Nazification?"[373]

Burger decided that the film would include footage from the various camps within a frame story that would show how it was possible for the Germans to tolerate the horrors of the Third Reich; he would present it as something that evolved slowly from the early days of German fascism. At that time, the Germans had failed to protest when they saw a neighbor brutalized by Brownshirts (SA, or Storm Troopers), even though this was a time when preventive action was still possible. Then he would show how, a little later, the Germans were happy to take over the Jewish businesses and Jewish homes that had been so suddenly vacated, how they welcomed the loot sent to them from the conquered countries, how they themselves "marched, guarded prisoners, carted them away, executed them. How they then sat in their cellars or in the trenches outside Stalingrad, and how they then said, they didn't know about anything."[374]

When Burger got to London, he learned that the film people work-

---

[372] Author interview with Albert Rosenberg, 6 Jan. 2014. Rosenberg said that he was able to use this pass even as late as the Johnson administration, when he requisitioned office space for his anti-poverty work in Ohio.

[373] Hanuš Burger, *Der Frühling war es wert*, 233.

[374] Hanuš Burger, *Der Frühling war es wert, 233.*

ing for the Office of War Information had quite a different concept of the film. They told him the film should, at most, be twenty minutes long, and that there should be no new filming but simply an editing together of some of the camp footage already in existence. For two weeks Burger spent three to five hours daily viewing the films of the concentration camps. It was a horrible experience. In his memoirs he would write:

> When I have a nightmare now, over thirty years later, I see the bulldozer of Bergen-Belsen, that again and again drives into the piles of soil and body parts and pushes them forwards; I see smoke-blackened chimneys, balls of hair, mountains of false teeth, shoes, prostheses, cleanly sorted, piled up, recorded in lists. [...]
> And back then I could not imagine that there would be people in Germany thirty years later who maintain, that Auschwitz never existed.[375]

Burger tried to explain to his American superiors that it "was not a matter of putting together a sleek, compelling flick that could fill out the program between the weekly news and the main feature, but rather a matter of a necessary, bitter medicine."[376] He was finally able to persuade the army to let him film some scenes in Germany that would demonstrate the German attitude towards the victims in the camps. But everything changed after America dropped the bomb on Hiroshima and Nagasaki in what Burger called "the greatest mass murder in world history."[377]

Now the Office of War Information brought in Billy Wilder to take over the production of the film. Wilder had already been to Weimar and filmed some documentary footage at Buchenwald.[378] Still, Burger was concerned: Wilder was, to be sure, a fine Hollywood director, but he had sat out the war in California and, Burger believed, was unable to grasp all the horror that had unfolded in Europe. Wilder cut Burger's raw film footage from seven thousand to twelve hundred feet,

---

[375] Hanuš Burger, *Der Frühling war es wert*, 237.
[376] Hanuš Burger, *Der Frühling war es wert*, 239.
[377] Hanuš Burger, *Der Frühling war es wert*, 252.
[378] David Hackett notes that by the time Billy Wilder arrived, "conditions at the camp were no longer as severe as they had been at liberation." *The Buchenwald Report*, 13.

with instructions that the film should inspire "shock—tears—shock again, and then at the end a sedative, saying that such a thing cannot happen again, with Eisenhower and Churchill and Truman, and, for all I care, Stalin as guarantee."[379] Wilder reduced the footage of the concentration camps, and left out the question of the average German's guilt, saying, "Objectively speaking, no matter how disagreeable [the Germans] are, they are still—and I now am citing verbatim our Uncle in Washington—our logical allies of tomorrow. And we cannot alienate them."[380] Burger's one consolation was that his Camp Sharpe friend and colleague Oskar Seidlin would still write the commentary for the film.[381]

Although the Office of War Information now dictated that the Germans were not to be alienated, Burger was somewhat mollified when he saw the final cut of *The Death Mills* [*Die Todesmühlen*]. He was especially pleased that the film sparked a vigorous discussion among the Germans with whom he saw it: while most still insisted that they had known nothing of the camps, Burger was gratified to see how a young German woman insisted that they had. Burger was also pleased that Wilder included in his film the sobering visit of the Weimar citizens to Buchenwald.

As for the people being held in the concentration camps, the Americans eventually gave them food packets and train passes so that they might return to their homes. When he was filming scenes for *The Death Mills* in Germany, Burger had already seen how these former concentration camp inmates were welcomed when they reached their home towns: "The villagers openly showed their hostility. They didn't like the [American] occupiers—and the former prisoners even less, although they didn't dare to say anything. And we were supposed to show the poignantly-happy return of a man discharged from a concentration camp?"[382]

The horror of the camps was bad enough, but the MRB men found the Americans' willingness to de-emphasize the question of collective

---

[379] Hanuš Burger, *Der Frühling war es wert*, 257.
[380] Hanuš Burger, *Der Frühling war es wert*, 259.
[381] In his memoirs, Burger stresses his own importance and Wilder's lack of qualifications to make a film that would do justice to the horrors of the camps. In reality, Wilder trimmed Burger's staged footage from the film and concentrated on the camps rather than on the didactic scenes Burger considered so important to the project.
[382] Hanuš Burger, *Der Frühling war es wert*, 249.

German guilt—or even German responsibility—especially disappointing. It looked to many of them that the unrepentant Germans might be right: that the United States and Britain would be more concerned with what they perceived as the rising threat of the Soviet Union than with a defeated Germany, and that they would enroll the Germans in their cause. This appeared to be confirmed by actions taken by the American Military Government. "If only the gentlemen of the AMG [...] would just use their own handbook!" Heym exclaimed. "But they don't. Instead they develop [...] an uncanny ability to select Nazis, or at the very least people who think like Nazis, for precisely the most important administrative posts."[383] They were already doing this, he added, in the winter and spring of 1945, before the Germans had even surrendered to the Allies. Still, even as some of the MRB men were becoming disillusioned with America's new military policies, most remained hopeful that they could help achieve reform through their own contributions to postwar Germany.

---

[383] Stefan Heym, *Nachruf*, 364-365.

Chapter 8

Going "Home"

There came no sound from inside the house. My heart sank. Had I come here, all the way from Prague—from America—to find only that it was too late? [...] Millions of people in Europe have vanished in the past years. Just vanished into thin air. No one will ever know what had happened to them, where they went, when they died. They were your parents and children and brothers and friends, and now you can't even put a bunch of fresh field flowers on their graves because they have no graves. They were not permitted the luxury of a simple grave in the earth that once was theirs.[384]

Joseph Wechsberg's hometown of Moravská-Ostrava lies in what is now the northeast corner of the Czech Republic. It was firmly under Russian control in the autumn of 1945, but Wechsberg (4th MRB company) went there anyway, mostly as a favor to his wife. Two years before, she had received a Red Cross message from her parents saying: "We are all right. Love." Wechsberg knew how, in the past two years, Europe had been "slowly bleeding to death. Millions of people had died of war and torture and disease and starvation in those two years. More millions had vanished." He had also heard that there had been heavy fighting in his old hometown, and that it had been heavily damaged.[385]

In spite of his reservations about what he might find there, Wechsberg set out, alone, on the journey to his childhood home. He had grown up and gone to elementary and secondary school there, and, even when he had left home to study music and law in Prague and Vienna, he had returned each year to visit his mother. He had seen many bombed-out cities in Germany and knew what might await him, and he braced himself for what he might find in Moravská-Ostrava. He would go to the home of his parents-in-law and look for them. And, although he held out little hope, he would try to learn what had become of his own many friends and relatives. He had had a big family: his mother had had twelve brothers and sisters and his father's family

---

[384] Joseph Wechsberg, *Homecoming*, 64.
[385] Joseph Wechsberg, *Homecoming*, 6.

had also been very large.[386] Still, he had not been home in seven years. And, given all that had transpired in that time, "It seemed like seventy years, or maybe seven hundred years."[387]

Throughout his service in the armed services, Wechsberg had harbored the dream of the day when the American army would liberate his homeland. He had pictured young Czech women, dressed in their brightly colored native dress, running up to him to offer him flowers and kisses, much as the French women had done in Paris. However, Moravská-Ostrava had already been liberated by the Russians and was a firm part of the Russian zone when he got there. Whatever euphoria his townspeople felt upon their liberation had now dissipated and been replaced with hesitation and fear: "Groups of people crowded the sidewalks. They were hesitant, as though they were discouraged to look, breathe, live. [...] They had the half-starved, tired, shabby look that comes from six years of fear, malnutrition, overwork, and not being able to buy new clothes."[388]

Wechsberg's overwhelming impression was that everyone was "gray." The men's worn-out shirts and collars had turned from white to gray, because the people had no soap for washing them. Worse, "even their faces were gray, their cheeks and lips and the whites of their eyes. The grayness of hunger and disease. The young girls had an aged, sickly look. There were no cosmetics, no milk, no vitamins, and no time to take sunbaths."[389]

When Wechsberg reached his in-laws' house, he saw no sign of life there and no one answered his knock on the door. Finally, however, a face peered fearfully from an upstairs window; then, after they had recognized him, his in-laws appeared at the door, to welcome him "home." They were showing signs of severe malnutrition, but they were delighted to see him and to learn about their daughter. Wechsberg inquired about members of his own family, but they could tell him very little, as they had been living in their cellar for months.

> Gradually the story was pieced together. A story of suffering. Very few members of my family were accounted for. [...] Now the few ones alive were scattered all over the globe. Santiago de Chile, Riga, Bucharest, Tel Aviv, Singapore, Cuba, Sao

---

[386] Joseph Wechsberg, *Homecoming*, 44.
[387] Joseph Wechsberg, *Homecoming*, 3.
[388] Joseph Wechsberg, *Homecoming*, 42-43.
[389] Joseph Wechsberg, *Homecoming*, 42-43.

Paolo (Brazil), and Leamington Spa in England. The pitiless, crazy geography of survival.

The rest—a silent roll call of hunger, fear, deportation, persecution, torture, death...'[390]

Wechsberg's own home had been bombed, ironically enough, by an American bomber, and for a brief moment he felt resentment toward the airman who had needlessly destroyed a private residence. But he was more saddened by the attitudes of the people now living in his hometown. He saw how desperately the people jockeyed for advantage: one woman was trying to get better food rations on the basis that she had once been married to a Jew; one man was complaining that another had been given housing he felt was his due, because he had been in one of the worst of the camps, and the other man had been "only" in Dachau. He saw people lying about their politics when they spoke to him, adjusting their speech to the uniform they saw him wearing. Wechsberg admitted,

> I became over suspicious with everybody I met. I found myself treating an old friend with cold apprehension—trying to figure him out. It was unfair, yet I couldn't help it. I became almost obsessed with the notion that I mustn't act too friendly to anybody, not before I had proof that he had been on the right side.
>
> Yet I had no right to judge these people. While they had been subject to fear, sadism, persecution, I had been tucked away safely in America. How easy it is to be righteous and indignant when you are firmly entrenched behind security and comfort! Do I know how I would have acted under the same circumstances?[391]

Wechsberg left the town knowing that it was no longer his home, that "there was no bridge leading from the past to the present."[392]

Another Sharpe man who returned to his home in Czechoslovakia did it with quite another purpose in mind. Walter Kohner, also of the 4th MRB company, had had to leave his fiancée in Europe when he em-

---
[390] Joseph Wechsberg, *Homecoming*, 67.
[391] Joseph Wechsberg, *Homecoming*, 95.
[392] Joseph Wechsberg, *Homecoming*, 117.

igrated to the United States, and he was desperate to find her. About one month after the German surrender, a letter reached him, saying that his fiancée had been liberated from the camps and that she was alive. Kohner got permission from his company commander to go at once to his hometown of Teplice (Teplitz), where Kohner believed his beloved Hanna might now be living. He was given the necessary papers for entering the Russian zone, issued a jeep and a driver from the motor pool, and set out for Teplice with his friend, Fred Perutz, who went along in order to determine the state of his father's old textile factory there.[393]

Outside Carlsbad, Kohner's jeep skidded on a rainy road and overturned. Kohner was not badly hurt, but the jeep was irreparably damaged. And Fred Perutz was seriously injured, with deep gashes to his face and leg. He had to remain behind. Kohner managed to get a small Czech vehicle and continue on his journey to Teplice. The drive there was sobering:

> The trip took hours. Not only was I still shaken but the roads were clogged with refugees. There were Sudeten Germans who were fleeing the Czechs, trying to get into Germany. There were Czechs trying to return to their homes. There were former inmates of concentration camps who were swept along in both directions, seemingly without destinations. There were detachments of Russian soldiers who were trying to bring some order to the chaos. People were using any kind of transportation: carts, horses, trucks, ancient automobiles and their own feet.[394]

Kohner had the same experience as Wechsberg, when he rang the bell at his fiancée's old home: no one answered, but he noticed a movement behind the window curtains. There was no happy reunion with in-laws, however; the house was now in another's hands. Kohner's own home was badly damaged: the windows were broken, part of the home's exterior stucco had fallen from the walls, and the garden and its gazebo were gone. Kohner remembered that his mother had had to leave her few remaining pieces of jewelry behind when she had left for the States, and that she had buried them by a lilac bush in the garden. Kohner went to the yard after dark, and dug up the

---

[393] Author interview with Fred Perutz, 1 Oct. 2013.
[394] Hanna and Walter Kohner, *Hanna and Walter*, 198.

strongbox. On examining the contents, he commented, "They were of no great value. But for her they belonged to a happier past."[395] After learning from a police official that, to the best of his knowledge, "none of the Jews who had lived in Teplice had returned,"[396] Kohner visited his father's grave, then returned to Carlsbad.

Fred Perutz, in the meantime, had his own unusual adventure. He had come through the war unscathed, but now his leg required surgery. This was performed, in Carlsbad, by an SS surgeon working under the supervision of a Russian officer. After the surgery, this officer begged Perutz to take him out of the Russian zone to the West. Of course, Perutz couldn't do that. As for his father's textile factory, Perutz learned that it had been converted into an airplane factory during the war; it had been bombed and was now a ruin.[397]

Like Joseph Wechsberg, Stefan Heym made a brief pilgrimage home, even though he knew that he would find no family here. He went to the Jewish cemetery, as Walter Kohner had, to find the grave of his father. But the Nazis in Chemnitz, a city in Saxony in eastern Germany, had been much more thorough then those in Teplice; they had knocked over all the Jewish headstones so that they lay face down, and it was impossible for Heym to find his father's grave. "And so he took a position in front of some ravished grave or other and, with his hand at his helmet, gave a respectful salute to his father and to all of the dead buried there."[398] Heym visited his childhood home, where nothing remained in the house interior to bring back memories of his former life there. He also went to the house he'd been born in—"Only the front wall is standing, someone has written a 13 in chalk next to the entrance which leads nowhere"—and had his driver take a picture of himself standing by the empty doorway. He also visited his old school, now a German hospital, and finally went to the site of the town synagogue:

> It takes a minute or two, before he realizes why he cannot find the temple: the temple is gone, there is no stone left of it, no fragment of brick; grass proliferates where the building once stood [...]; they have burned the temple and cleared away

---

[395] Hanna and Walter Kohner, *Hanna and Walter*, 201.
[396] Hanna and Walter Kohner, *Hanna and Walter*, 199.
[397] Author interview with Fred Perutz, 1 Oct. 2013.
[398] Stefan Heym, *Nachruf*, 355.

the charred ruins; now the city itself has become a landscape of ruins and only here is green life flourishing.[399]

Heym's driver tried to console him for the eradication of his life there: "Don't take it so hard; after all, we won."[400]

Stefan Heym had no expectation of meeting up with friends or family in Chemnitz and he had no confrontations with the local citizens. Curt Jellin, also from the 2nd MRB, had quite a different experience when he returned to the Ruhr district and his hometown of Herne. He was also more burdened than Heym had been by frightful memories from his past. As a boy, he had never experienced much anti-Semitism. But, on April 1st, 1933, during a boycott of Jewish stores in Cologne, Jellin had been recognized as a Jew and ordered to carry a banner reading "We Jews are your misfortune." When he threw the banner to the ground he was given a savage beating by some SS men. They knocked his teeth out, kicked him viciously in the stomach, and then forced him to take the banner and carry it through the streets while onlookers followed him, spitting and kicking out at him. Two days later, he landed in the hospital for an operation on his stomach.[401]

Jellin came back to Herne not knowing exactly what had happened to his parents, but fearing the worst. When he discovered that two notoriously sadistic anti-Semites were now living in his parents' apartment, he lost control. He shoved his way in past the woman who answered the door, and began wrecking the apartment. When the woman's husband returned, he asked him what had happened to the Jews who had lived there. The man said:

> "The Jellins, they all went to the United States." I said, "you liar"—and I took him along—I put him in the staff car and I took him out of town and [...] did something to him—I was in the mood to knock him off. [...]. But I didn't have the nerve because first of all this was British territory and they even approached me—a British officer who said, "You are not here in Russia. You are not allowed to do this."
>
> [...] So I had him arrested and they kept him for a certain time and [then] the British let him go. He was a living beast—

---

[399] Stefan Heym, *Nachruf*, 355.
[400] Stefan Heym, *Nachruf*, 355.
[401] Curt Jellin interview with Rosalyn Manowitz.

this guy. And I found out what happened to my father and mother. They were supposed to be sent to a concentration camp. They weren't sent [there]. It was the last shipment because my father was a front soldier and with another man who was a doctor in town and was a medical doctor during the first World War—they were put on a cattle train and the train was taken out of Herne and it was sealed and the whole car was gassed. That was their end.[402]

Like Curt Jellin, Ernst Cramer of the 2nd MRB company had good reason to hurry back to his hometown of Augsburg, in southern Bavaria. Upon his release from Buchenwald seven years earlier, Cramer had had to leave Germany; now he returned to Augsburg, to look for news of what had happened to his father, mother, and brother Erwin. In February 1944 the proud old city, that boasted of being twice as old as Nuremberg or Munich, had suffered severe damage in an Allied air attack on the Messerschmidt weapons factory and the main railroad station. Almost a quarter of the homes in Augsburg and a large section of the historic district had been destroyed. Cramer said that the darkest moment of his wartime experiences was, "When I returned to Augsburg at the beginning of May 1945 as an American soldier and ascertained that my parents really had been taken away; already then I feared that they were dead."[403] Cramer learned that after the family had been taken away from their home, the family cook had found a piece of paper on the table with a five line poem written by Ernst Cramer's father: "The song is finished. True, the melodies still ring softly in the house. But it is over. The song is finished."[404]

In a bitterly ironic twist, Ernst Cramer was in Augsburg on the day that Germany surrendered to the Allied forces. Cramer would later remind the people of Augsburg of their guilt in the deaths of their Jewish neighbors:

> Naturally there were [...] those—here in Augsburg as well as everyplace in Germany—who were opposed, who did not collaborate, who tried to help, who even offered resistance. But they were just far too few. The majority turned their backs.

---

[402] Curt Jellin interview with Rosalyn Manowitz.
[403] "Ich will nicht verdrängen!" *Bild*, 28 Jan. 2013.
[404] Cited in "Around the Jewish World: Germany's Past and Future Reflected in Honor for German Jewish Journalist," *JTA*.

Enough were active participants and took part in the injustice, in the injustice that began with so-called petty details and wound up with murder. These collaborators, these facilitators of injustice—and this remains totally incomprehensible—were folks from next door, in our case from Augsburg and Bavaria.

The policemen that picked up my parents and my brother from their home in the Maximilianstrasse on Maundy Thursday 1942 were Augsburgers.

The bus driver who drove them to some railroad track or other was an Augsburger. The men who then shoved them into compartments of railroad cars in Munich, and who later prodded them into boxcars were Germans.[405]

It was because of the non-collaborators that Cramer chose to remain in Germany. He pledged the remainder of his life to memorialize what had happened during the Nazi years and to "revive in Germany the ideals of liberty, of freedom, of self-determination, simply of democracy."[406] And he, like so many of the survivors of Nazi Germany, would be tormented for the remainder of his life with survivor's guilt, saying, "Not a day has gone by in all these decades that I have not thought of my parents, of my brother, with a mixture of pain, melancholy, and guilt, including self-recriminations such as, 'Why did I not do more to try to save them?' or 'Why was I allowed to survive instead of them?'"[407]

Albert Rosenberg did not return to his old hometown of Göttingen to search for family members, but took his SHAEF jeep, instead, and drove to Bergen-Belsen, the concentration camp near Celle, in the British zone, because he had heard that several of his relatives had been sent there. It was, Rosenberg recounted, one of the saddest days of his life:

> I drove through the camp, through that horrible death, people lying there staring into space, shouting on my U.S.

---

[405] Ernst Cramer, "Address for the Convocation of a Memorial Tablet for the Jewish Victims of Nazism from Augsburg."

[406] Ernst Cramer, "Standing Together—Opening remarks by Professor Ernst Cramer at the 59th Convention."

[407] Ernst Cramer, "Address for the Convocation of a Memorial Tablet for the Jewish Victims of Nazism from Augsburg."

Army bullhorn, screaming out to see if anyone knew the Rosenberg family from Göttingen. I found no one. Later I met one of my relatives, my cousin Henry, one of the few who survived—twenty-eight died—and he told me he heard me. He heard me shouting! But he could barely move. He couldn't answer my call.[408]

Rosenberg did not even consider staying on in Germany after the war. He sometimes thought that the true story of his life was trying to "outrun evil," "to stay one step ahead." Decades later, recalling his own near-death experiences at the hands of Nazi thugs—the near fatal beating in Göttingen, the encircling by Nazi murderers at the POW camp near Metz—, Rosenberg commented: "It might sound silly, that a ninety-year-old man would be dying from the effects of a beating that took place in 1937, but it is true, both physiologically and metaphorically. This pain has been inside me since that day."[409]

Peter Wyden would make it his mission after the war to try to understand how it was that a person could become so evil as to send hundreds of fellow citizens, including one's own friends, to certain death. He was stationed in his hometown of Berlin after the war as the Berlin bureau chief of Habe's newspaper *Die Neue Zeitung*. On March 17, 1946, while glancing through the equivalent paper put out by the Soviets for their occupied German territories, he was stunned to learn that an old Jewish school chum of his, one Stella Goldschlag, had played a horrific role in the Jewish holocaust: she had hunted down hundreds of Berlin Jews and turned them over to the Gestapo for arrest and deportation. Now she herself was on trial in the Russian zone. Wyden was shocked at this revelation, but chose, at the time, not to mention what he'd learned to any of his friends:

> The revelations about Stella were as revolting to me as the photos of the corpses in the camps. They were also personally upsetting. I felt dirtied by her works. To have shared the same classroom with Stella was suddenly embarrassing, like having once had a cheery dinner with a rapist. That's why I didn't want to talk about her at the time. Her unmasking was too re-

---

[408] Cited in Mark Jacobson, *The Lampshade*, 163.
[409] Mark Jacobson, *The Lampshade*, 170.

cent, too raw a wound.[410]

He did not forget her story, however. He learned that she had been sentenced to ten years of hard labor in a Russian prison camp. After she was released from the camp, she was put on trial in the West, once in 1957 and again in 1972. Wyden followed these trials; he also talked with everyone he could find who could report about the situation in Berlin under the Nazis and about Stella's role as a betrayer of her fellow Jews, among them many of Stella's former friends and classmates. Finally, in 1992, Wyden wrote her story. It is an unusual, objective look at someone who not only became an apparent supporter of Hitler, but played a pivotal role in the Nazis' genocide program. It is a rare document about the corruption of a German Jew forced to live with fear and self-hatred in Hitler's Germany.

What made Stella act as she did? Wyden comes up with several intriguing theories. One was her own desperate desire to be taken as an Aryan herself. Shapely, blond, blue-eyed, and remarkably attractive, Stella did not resemble the stereotypical hook-nosed Jew pictured in the anti-Semitic propaganda put out by the Nazis. She appeared willing to do almost anything to avoid being associated with the loathsome "vermin" described by Hitler's propaganda machine.

Second, she had been arrested and tortured by the Gestapo. She was terrified and desperate to preserve her life and those of her parents, who were being held hostage to her actions: as long as she participated in hunting down Jews, they would be held in Berlin and not transported to a death camp.

Stella, however, remained an active participant in the hunt for German Jews even after her parents were deported. This raises questions that are difficult to answer. Was she too deeply immersed by that time to pull back from these betrayals? Was this a case of what is now known as the "Stockholm syndrome"? Or was she simply convinced that this was the only way she could possibly preserve her own life?

Wyden raises several interesting points. One is Stella's own statement that the Americans were worse than Hitler in their betrayal of the Jews. Her family had tried to flee Germany, but the United States not only kept its quota for Jewish immigrants extremely low, but they seldom filled even these quotas. Again and again roadblocks were put in the way of those seeking an escape route. In the summer of 1939,

---

[410] Peter Wyden, *Stella*, 243.

Stella's first husband had been on the *S.S. St. Louis*, whose captain had anchored off shore from Cuba and then just off the Florida coast in hopes of gaining entry for over 900 refugee Jews. The United States took none of them, and the ship returned to Europe. Stella's husband and his parents were sent back to Germany and perished in the Nazi death camps.

Wyden also points out that countless Jews cooperated to at least some degree with the Gestapo's roundups and confinements of their friends and neighbors. Sometimes this was done for humanitarian reasons, in order to provide a modicum of better treatment for people who would be seized and imprisoned anyway, sometimes for the more selfish desire for self-preservation. Wyden consulted a number of psychiatrists who specialized in extreme behavior. One asked, "What if she hadn't [cooperated]? Wouldn't she have been sent to a concentration camp? If I'd been in that situation, I'd have done it too. It all depends on the kind of situation we're in."[411] Another commented, "Her potential for evil was tapped and cultivated"; the Gestapo had drawn her in by "promising safety for herself and her parents, and then snapping the trap shut."[412]

In 1990 and 1991, Wyden paid three visits to Stella. He found her living the life of a recluse, and in full denial of her crimes. Still he found great hope for the future among many of the survivors and especially among the second-generation survivors whom he interviewed. "The emotional fallout of the Holocaust," he said, "had given rise to a crop of curiously strong, humanitarian descendants, a little-noted and paradoxical outcome."[413] For Wyden, as for Ernst Cramer, people like Stella Goldschlag, the cowed citizens of Moravská-Ostrava, the anti-Semites of Herne and Augsburg, the SS officers at Buchenwald and Bergen-Belsen, were figures from Germany's horrific past. Their strong and altruistic children were its future.

---

[411] Peter Wyden, *Stella*, 297.
[412] Peter Wyden, *Stella*, 311.
[413] Peter Wyden, *Stella*, 332.

Chapter 9

Working for a Democratic Germany

> *"Look here, gentlemen, in this last year and a half I have interrogated many hundreds of your countrymen. Practically every one of them has, indeed, asserted that he knew nothing of the camps. But whenever he was cornered and had to speak out about his Nazi past, then suddenly every one of these heroes had his private Jewish, social democratic or communist friend, whom he personally hid or otherwise saved. Saved from what? Can you tell me that, gentlemen? From a fine for violating a no parking zone—or from the gas chambers of Auschwitz?"*[414]

Even after Germany's unconditional surrender on May 7, 1945, many of the Sharpe soldiers continued their wartime assignments, with the main difference being that these activities were now primarily directed to German civilians. The MRB companies had been dissolved. The PWD—Psychological Warfare Department—was replaced by the ICD—Information Control Division; it was under the leadership of Robert A. McClure, former head of the PWD. This new ICD controlled cultural affairs in those parts of Germany under the governance of the U.S. military. Colonel Clifford R. Powell, formerly commanding officer of the Psychological War Service Battalion, 12th Army Group, was now deputy chief of the ICD's operations branch. Hence the Sharpe men's superiors remained the same, despite the shift in the U.S. Army from warfare to military governance of Germany. Those former MRB men who still had time left to serve in the army continued to serve, but their duties shifted from wartime propaganda to de-Nazification and re-education in the American democratic tradition. They helped recreate a German press, reestablish broadcasting capabilities, and interrogate German civilians requesting licensure in education, media, and the arts.

Just as Hans Habe had set up the German section of Radio Luxembourg prior to the Battle of the Bulge, so he now took over the establishment of the first German newspapers published under U.S. Army auspices. Until a free, democratic German press could be entrusted

---

[414] Hanuš Burger, *Der Frühling war es wert*, 265.

with publishing newspapers, Habe and his men would provide the news. Working with a small group of trusted collaborators, many of them men who had worked with Radio Luxembourg—men such as Stefan Heym, Peter Wyden, Konrad Kellen, Joseph Wechsberg, Max Kraus, and Joseph Eaton[415]—Habe set up a system whereby a new newspaper appeared almost as soon as a German city had fallen. Soon there were eighteen papers under his supervision, with names such as *Frankfurter Presse*, the *Bayrischer Tag*, the *Weser-Bote*, the *Kölnischer Kurier*, the *Hessische Post*, the *Ruhr-Bote*, the *Regensburger Post*, and the *Augsburger Anzeiger*. Habe noted with some pride that, "At the peak of our activity the total circulation of our papers topped eight million: it was the world's second biggest newspaper concern."[416] Because only a few of Habe's men were professional journalists, Habe gave them all a crash course in newspaper layout and writing styles. As he had done in his instruction at Camp Sharpe, Habe showed the men that these papers must be created according to strict German standards; for example, the top story of the week must be carried in the upper left-hand corner, instead of the upper right, as in American papers.[417] Habe had the men learn the differences in attitude and in writing in the European press, such as the tendency to condense quoted speeches, to use occasional partial sentences, and to avoid descriptions of people and their immediate environment. Habe even covered the matter of headlines, telling his men that, whereas American headlines tended to condense a story, European headlines merely provided a "window" into it. In America, he said, sub-headings gave more details of the story, but in Europe subheadings were designed simply to make the story more appealing. A box on the front page of a European paper was to be reserved for news flashes, and never used simply for a feature. Max Kraus recalled:

> There were no news wires operating in Germany, so everything came out from Habe's office in Bad Nauheim. He had a monitoring unit to [track] Voice of America broadcasts,

---

[415] Others working on these papers included Otto Brand (2nd MRB Company), Kurt Wittler (3rd), Louis Atlas (4th), and, from the 5th: Roderick Fruendt, Gerhard Speyer, Erwin Strauß [Irvin Straus?], Kurt Wittler, and Ernst Wynder. See Eva-Juliane Welsch, *Die hessischen Lizenzträger und ihre Zeitungen*, 29.
[416] Hans Habe, *All My Sins*, 352.
[417] *PWB Combat Team...*, 53.

BBC, and any other stations they could find, transcribe them, and submit them to Habe, where they were turned into the bulk of the copy for these newspapers.

Once a week a courier—either in a Jeep, or sometimes we used light planes—brought this copy to the various cities where [...] these weekly papers were being published. During the interval between the publication of one issue and the other issue, we American editors also had to gather the news to add a local page or local part to the papers.

[...] Then, the local news, that we had gathered in our local papers, was taken back to Bad Nauheim by the courier. That was the basis for the domestic German news for the next issue of all the papers. It was quite an amazing operation.[418]

In addition, "since the copy that we got from Bad Nauheim was probably at least twelve hours old since the time it had been written," Max Kraus and the other editors had to monitor the latest Voice of America or BBC newscast to make sure that nothing had happened in the meantime that would affect the stories in the papers.[419] Habe commented that what critics liked to call "The Habe Empire" had the distinction of having more papers than it did editorial staff. Max Kraus, for example, was responsible for two newspapers: one for Munich, and one for Augsburg. Habe remarked:

I might have made things simpler for myself, but I made a point of 'camouflaging' identical news in such a way that each paper looked entirely different from the other and had a really new look. Thus, through my different handling of type size and headlines, I produced the *Frankfurter Presse* as a serious daily and the *Bayrischer Tag*, printed in Bamberg, as a popular tabloid. This was an attempt to demonstrate different kinds of newspapers and to avoid a sense of regimentation.[420]

While Habe set up the newspapers that covered the gap between the German surrender and the establishment of German-run newspapers published by politically pure Germans, other Sharpe men were busy reestablishing radio programming in the new American zone.

---

[418] Max W. Kraus interview with Cliff Groce.
[419] Max W. Kraus interview with Cliff Groce.
[420] Hans Habe, *All My Sins*, 352-353.

The broadcasting units took over the various radio studios and transmitters, and put them back on the air using MRB personnel. T/4 Owen Lehr and his colleagues of the 5th MRB company helped reactivate the Frankfurt am Main broadcast station;[421] Captain Louis Muhlbauer and T/5 Philip Pines reactivated the station in Bremen.

Another group of former Sharpe men worked as interrogators in America's de-Nazification program. They began interviewing German civilians to gauge the degree to which they had served the Nazi cause. The interrogators determined which professors, theater personnel, artists, musicians, and publishers should receive a license to practice their trade in the new Germany. They also determined which civilians should be punished.

They often found these interrogations frustrating, since nearly everyone claimed to have been unsupportive of the Nazi regime all along. Albert Rosenberg held one of the strangest interrogations when he stumbled across Prince August Wilhelm, son of Germany's last emperor, living in a castle in a rural setting near Frankfurt am Main.[422] Rosenberg knew that the prince, popularly known as "Auwi," had been an extremely early and enthusiastic supporter of Hitler, even to the extent of joining the Nazi party in 1930 and introducing Hitler at early party rallies. The prince, however, felt entitled to special treatment, through his blood ties both to the royal house of Britain, and to Louis Mountbatten, the Supreme Allied Commander of the South East Asia Command. Rosenberg arrested the prince, and "Auwi" was cooperative until he was led to the Jeep. He then became unruly, and Rosenberg had to tie his hands behind his back in order to control him. "Imagine," Rosenberg exclaimed, "I, an American officer and a German Jew, tying the hands of a Prussian prince!"[423] When Auwi continued to resist his captors, Rosenberg's driver pulled down the prince's pants to prevent his flight. Once in Frankfurt, Rosenberg had to wait for three days for the Americans to take the prince off his hands. During these days, Rosenberg interrogated him in a dingy hotel room in Frankfurt. Here the prince, who still bore the rank of lieutenant general in the storm troopers (SA), even though he had fallen out of favor

---

[421] Owen A. Lehr, "Ham Radio in Europe After V-J Day," *QCWA JOURNAL*, Summer 1995, 47.

[422] Kronberg. The castle belonged to the prince's aunt Margaret, Countess of Hessen.

[423] Albert Rosenberg interview with Sylvia Cohen, Tape 3.

with the party in 1942, uttered the ridiculous phrase, "Ich bin nur ein kleines Würstchen" (I am just small fry). "I interviewed him," Rosenberg remembers, "just to see what made him tick." He soon discovered that the prince "was such a meaningless person" that he "made no impression."[424]

One of the men from Rosenberg's interrogation unit, Richard Akselrad, was given the task of interviewing Germany's Catholic bishops, to determine the reasons behind the Church's mostly passive compliance with the Nazi regime. Even those who had, to some degree, spoken out against the Nazi death camps, were defensive in their answers. Bishop Albert Stohr of Mainz, who had, in his sermons, spoken against Nazi violence, told Akselrad, that the survivors of the German concentration camps had shown no more courage than the bishops whom they were now criticizing. "Most of them," he protested, "were thrown in concentration camps against their will as a result of indirect utterances and secret actions. [...] Many of them became victims of their own imprudence and rashness which have nothing to do with courage." And Josef Frings, Archbishop of Cologne and an outspoken critic of Hitler and Nazism, asked Akselrad, "Who has the right to demand that the bishops should have chosen a form of fight that would have sent them to the gallows with infallible certainty, and which would have resulted in a campaign of extermination against the church?"[425]

The American interrogators found such defensiveness typical. Edward Alexander, of the 5th MRB company, remembers his interrogation of the great concert pianist Walter Gieseking:

> Prior to my interrogation, Gieseking gave a piano recital for the American troops, performing traditional music. But what followed at its end stands out in my memory. He asked his audience to call out composers they wished to hear, and among the several shouted was "Mendelssohn." Gieseking performed short pieces by Chopin, Schumann and Beethoven—ignoring Mendelssohn. Several days later when he sat before me, I asked him about the omission—was there any reason? He became uncomfortable, then went into a long explana-

---

[424] Author interview with Albert Rosenberg, 13 Jan. 2014. When the prince was tried by an American court in 1948, he was sentenced to time served.

[425] Cited in James Bernauer, "The Holocaust and the Catholic Church's Search for Forgiveness."

tion, pointing out that there wasn't enough time to include all the suggestions from the audience. I persisted—could it be because of the Nazi rejection of Mendelssohn because of his ethnic heritage? More discomfort, then after a recounting of his great popularity and success in his U.S. tours he said—"I was never a Nazi follower. I was like Furtwängler who never gave the Nazi salute, even when Hitler went to his concerts, but retained Jewish musicians in the Philharmonic."[426] I still pursued my questioning by asking how he felt about Goebbels' decision to ask Carl Orff to write new music for "Midsummer Night's Dream" to replace Mendelssohn's brilliant and famous score. Gieseking became visibly upset—and did not reply.[427]

Benno Frank, who now served as Chief of the Theater and Music section of the military government, declared:

> Only a few people outside of Germany were familiar with political leaders like Hess, Ley, Ribbentrop, etc., but artists like Richard Strauss, Gerhart Hauptmann, and Wilhelm Furtwängler were internationally known and recognized. Today it may be said that Hitler's success in using these prominent cultural figures has decisively contributed to the prestige of the Nazi Regime.[428]

As interrogators, the Sharpe men had remarkable leeway in granting or withholding approval to applicants for licenses. Ernst Cramer recalled:

---

[426] Wilhelm Furtwängler, Germany's most famous conductor, was cleared of all charges in his de-Nazification trial, since he had, provably, spoken out against Nazi anti-Semitism and refused to conduct in German-occupied countries. He ultimately fled to Switzerland before the end of the war.

[427] Edward Alexander, letter to author, 3 Oct. 2013. Gieseking was, like many German artists, blacklisted for a time, but by January 1947 the U.S. military government cleared him. His planned concert tour of the United States in January 1949 had to be cancelled, however, because of protests by veterans and by the Anti-Defamation League. His first official visit to the States was in 1953, where he played to a sold-out audience at Carnegie Hall.

[428] Benno Frank, "Theater and Music as a Principle Part of Re-orientation in Germany," 16 Sept. 1947. Cited in Abby Anderton, "'It was never a Nazi Orchestra': The American Re-education of the Berlin Philharmonic."

Some day rather early in the game I refused a certain person to become a licensed newspaper-editor. A first survey-team, which had checked the man, remonstrated: "This man was investigated thoroughly; he never was a Nazi."

I retorted, saying: "It is true, he is certainly not only a non-Nazi, but an Anti-Nazi. But he also is not a democrat; his ideas are totalitarian, autocratic. He hates any form of private ownership."

The man was a convinced communist.[429]

As an interrogator, Samson B. Knoll was assigned the duties of "Chief Interrogator for Military Government Information Control" of the Army administration in Marburg from May 1945 until the end of August. The town, much renowned for the excellence of its university, had not been bombed in the war, and Knoll settled in to the task of making decisions regarding the licensing of the city's media, cultural and university staffing. His work, he said, actually had less to do with control than with the discovery whether applicants for cultural licenses "were really what they said. Most said, of course: We were never Nazis. Or they said: We were forced, and so on." But, with access to the total archives of the German Reich's Cultural and Literary Chambers, Knoll could easily point out the discrepancies between what applicants said about themselves and what the records showed they had done. "For, if somebody comes to me and says, I was always anti-Nazi, and never cooperated, and I discover that he paid dues to the SS, then that does not speak well for his sense of truthfulness."[430]

In his discussions with faculty members at the university Knoll met with attitudes that were probably typical of those held at many German universities of the day: that the university had not been politically involved with the Hitler regime because the university had a "purely intellectual mission." Knoll's "objection was, that it was this purely intellectual attitude of the university that was its undoing."[431] Still, Knoll found only a handful of university faculty who had been pro-Hitler activists during the Nazi regime, while "all the others were

---

[429] Ernst Cramer, "Standing Together—Opening remarks."
[430] Walter Bernsdorff and Martin Vialon, "Vom Um-Erzieher zum Freund," 30.
[431] Walter Bernsdorff and Martin Vialon, "Vom Um-Erzieher zum Freund," 35.

people who really and truly had been in the inner resistance."[432]

Like many other former MRB men, Knoll was disturbed that the American occupying forces did not always live up to their own higher standard. "It was always my position," he said, "that we Americans had a duty to show the Germans that we appreciated the difference between Nazis, and Non-Nazis, and Anti-Nazis [...]. And that this should be shown in our public treatment of them."[433] When a new U.S. army unit came into Marburg, and one of its officers tried to confiscate the home of the theologian Rudolf Bultmann, Knoll sprang into action. Knoll knew that, in 1935, Bultmann had led a protest of the university's theology department against the implementation of the anti-Semitic Nuremberg Laws, and he was outraged that Bultmann should be punished for this by losing his living quarters. Knoll drove to Army headquarters in Wiesbaden, and convinced the General to call and reverse the order.

Some of the American actions resulted from ignorance. When Albert Rosenberg was assigned to Bremen for interrogations of job applicants, he discovered that the American military government had already installed a large number of former Nazis in official functions simply because they spoke excellent English. Rosenberg learned that the Americans had even made Erich Vagts, who had served as a Nazi representative to Berlin, Minister President of the State of Bremen. Rosenberg informed SHAEF headquarters of this outrage, and Vagts was quickly removed from power. In the meantime, Rosenberg found some anti-Nazis who had been jailed by the Nazi officials in charge, and saw to it that they were released. He was particularly admiring of Fritz and Frieda Paul, who had worked against the Nazis by printing and distributing anti-Nazi leaflets during the 1930s. They had rejected the opportunity to leave Germany, and chose imprisonment, instead, because of the prospect that gave them of resuming their activities after their release.[434]

Several of the Sharpe men sprang into action when they saw the

---

[432] Walter Bernsdorff and Martin Vialon, "Vom Um-Erzieher zum Freund," 35.

[433] Walter Bernsdorff and Martin Vialon, "Vom Um-Erzieher zum Freund," 36.

[434] Albert Rosenberg interview with Sylvia Cohen, Tape 2.

need for it. Joseph Eaton,[435] of the 4th MRB company, was editor of the *Regensburger Post*, and was living in Straubing, where the press was located. He saw that the Straubing synagogue had been badly defaced by the local populace; it had not been burned only because it was part of a block of buildings, and the locals did not want to risk losing the other structures to fire. Eaton went to the mayor to get the names of the people who had participated in the synagogue's desecration. Then he made the female relatives of those people participate in cleaning up the synagogue and restoring it to its former condition.[436]

Eaton also paid a visit to Hitler's birthplace in the Austrian town of Braunau am Inn. The old home had been turned into a library. At Eaton's instigation, and with the assistance of the Straubing Catholic priest, a memorial exhibition about Hitler's atrocities and the Nazi concentration camps was opened there in November, 1945.[437]

Many of the Sharpe men disapproved of certain aspects of the U.S. military government being established in Germany. It seemed to them that all too few American officers made the fine distinction that Pastor Martin Niemöller made between Germany's "collective responsibility" and its "collective guilt," and that this meant that the Germans were treated in an undifferentiated manner. Nor were they pleased with the strict regulations against fraternization between German civilians and members of the U.S. military.[438]

Hans Habe even came into conflict with General Dwight D. Eisenhower over the content of the new newspaper that he had been called upon to edit for the U.S. zone in Germany. The paper was called *Die Neue Zeitung* [The New Newspaper] and had as its subheading "An American newspaper for the German population."

By the time Habe took over the editorship of this newspaper in October 1945, all but two of his regional papers had been given over,

---

[435] Joseph Eaton [Josef Wechsler], was born in Nuremberg, Germany. He was expelled from Berlin's Hohenzollern Gymnasium at age 14 for being a Jew. His parents sent him to New York under the auspices of the German-Jewish Children's Aid program to complete his education. He changed his family name to protect his parents from German retribution. He graduated from Cornell University in 1940.

[436] Joseph Eaton interview with Judith Cohen, 1 Aug. 2010, 82-83.

[437] Joseph Eaton interview with Judith Cohen, 1 Aug. 2010, 80-81.

[438] These regulations would be loosened by the end of 1945, after the war against Japan was over.

under license, to new, all-German staffs. Meanwhile, in recognition of his services, Habe had been promoted to Major. At his first meeting with Eisenhower, Habe was shocked at the General's demeanor:

> Platitudes, more and more horrifying to the officer who had at first been quite intimidated with admiration, were pronounced with the finality of Socratic wisdom.
> "We don't want to entertain the Germans," the General said, "but to instruct them. You've got to keep that in mind all the time."
> At last I pulled myself together to retort, "General, we can't force anybody to buy the *Neue Zeitung*. A paper can't help making concessions to its readers."
> "We aren't here to make concessions," the General replied impatiently.
> [...] At last, after about an hour during which he had given me instructions which no journalist could possibly have implemented, he demanded that I should take down his further observations verbatim. They were the personal message which, signed by himself, he wanted to see on the front page of the first issue.[439]

This statement read, in part:

> Militarism must be destroyed together with Nazism. Physical demilitarization is being actively implemented, but this alone is no guarantee that Germany may not at some future date drive the world into a new war. Military thinking must be eradicated from the German mind. Aggression is regarded as immoral by all the civilized nations of the world; the Germans have yet to be educated to grasp this obvious truth.[440]

In spite of Eisenhower's constraints, Habe managed, on the very presses the Nazis had used for their own national paper, to create postwar Germany's most popular newspaper. Habe hired Stefan Heym to be in charge of reporting on foreign affairs, and German author Erich Kästner to be in charge of the paper's feuilleton articles, even though the Information Control Division was not at all interested in having its

---

[439] Hans Habe, *All My Sins*, 361-362.
[440] Hans Habe, *All My Sins*, 362.

newspaper promote German culture. Most of the staffing from Habe's regional papers moved over to work on *Die Neue Zeitung*. The paper printed pieces by many of the best German thinkers and writers of the day: Theodor Adorno, Alfred Kerr, Luise Rinser, Martin Niemöller, Wolfgang Hildesheim, Thomas and Heinrich Mann. In addition the paper printed occasional booklets designed to teach the Germans American ways: *Jeder lernt Englisch* (English for Everyone), for example, or a 32-page booklet co-authored by Max Kraus called *Kleiner Kursus im Baseball-Spiel* (A Little Course in Baseball).

But Habe's idea of re-educating the Germans differed from that of the Military Government. Culturally, he saw two Germanies, one exemplary, one deplorable, and sought to promote the former in his newspaper. The ICD caused him frequent grief by insisting that at least one-third of the authors represented in its pages should be Americans and that the paper must adhere strictly to the U.S. program and policies.[441] In Habe's eyes, re-education failed in post-war Germany for two reasons: First, "because the victors, in their mania for collective guilt, would not entrust it to Germans"; and secondly, "because America was the only democratic country they knew, they believed that Americanism was the cure for Germany's ills." He objected to the Americans' equating "re-education" with "Americanization," and their defining "culture" as "popular culture"—instead of in the European sense of "higher culture."

Habe also felt that America too often failed to lead by example. Just as Knoll had to fight in Marburg to protect the true anti-Nazis from the vagaries of American officers, so Habe fought what he regarded as American hypocrisies:

> One could not re-educate a nation to justice and at the same time mock justice at Nuremberg; preach fair dealings and smuggle cigarettes; socially ostracize those to be re-educated and push the prices up in the prostitutes' market; condemn soldiers and re-employ Gestapo agents; or strip the police of their jackboots one day and put the demilitarized into those jackboots the next.[442]

---

[441] Habe cites an example of some military figure objecting to his printing of a piece by Carl Sandburg, since "the German public might take Sandburg for a German." *All My Sins*, 366.

[442] Hans Habe, *All My Sins*, 366.

At the same time that Habe was chafing against American policies he considered wrong for Germany, he antagonized some of his own Camp Sharpe protégés by openly criticizing actions taken by the Soviet Union. This alienated him from men like Stefan Heym and Hanuš Burger, who now openly broke with him, as well as with the American military authorities. It was a confusing time for America: Habe was instructed not to publish anything in *Die Neue Zeitung* that was critical of Russia; at the same time (1945), the House Un-American Activities Committee was made a permanent standing committee in Washington and began focusing its investigations on the activities of real and suspected communists in the United States. Stefan Heym was called back to the United States at the end of 1945 and discharged from the army because of his pro-communist leanings, but when Habe's deputy, Hans Wallenberg, printed an article in *Die Neue Zeitung* that was highly critical of Russian behavior in Silesia and in the Sudetenland, the military government reprimanded both Wallenberg and Habe for speaking ill of America's war-time ally.[443] Habe's situation became untenable, and, in 1949, he left his position at *Die Neue Zeitung* to try new ventures in Germany and the United States.

It was a period of political transition for the United States, and America's anti-Communist interests were beginning to overpower its anti-Fascist concerns. Questions of re-education and Germany's collective guilt gave way to a new policy that dictated that most Germans were free of Nazi tendencies. Re-education gave way to Cold War tensions.[444] Still, those who had worked with Habe on his newspapers could take pride in their influence on the new German press:

> *Die Neue Zeitung* [...] marked a milestone in the development of Germany's postwar press. It introduced the separation of news and commentary, today practiced by all West German dailies. It reintroduced German readers to the German and world literature that had been banned under Hitler. And most important, it trained a whole generation of young Germans

---

[443] Ironically, after Wallenberg took over the position of chief editor from Hans Habe, and anti-Communist furor raged in Washington, Hans Wallenberg would be accused of being pro-Communist and employing Communist members at *Die Neue Zeitung*. See "Bitterer Lorbeer," *Der Spiegel*, 30 Sept. 1953, 14.

[444] See Gienow-Hecht, *Transmission Impossible*, 7.

who, today, hold leading positions in journalism, public relations, and even politics.[445]

With the start of the Cold War, many Sharpe men had outlived their usefulness to the U.S. military, although some would continue working for *Die Neue Zeitung* and for the Voice of America. Konrad Kellen (2nd MRB) would work for Radio Free Europe. Arthur Bardos (4th MRB) would be called upon to direct a network of broadcasting stations in Austria; for a brief time Boris Kremenliev served as musical director of Radio Frankfurt, while Fred Lorenz later became program director there. Benno Frank served the U.S. military government until 1948 as Chief of Theatre and Music in Germany. Some found other places to serve in the U.S. Army: in the Panama Canal Zone (Gordon Frick), in Korea (Maxwell Grabove), and even in Saudi Arabia (Joseph Goularte).

During the Nuremberg Trials of major war criminals, Gunter Kosse served as interpreter for the lawyers conducting their preliminary investigations. As translator, Kosse took advantage of his knowledge of German culture in order to help the non-German-speaking lawyers phrase their questions in a manner conducive to obtaining information from such top Nazi officials as Ernst Kaltenbrunner, Fritz Sauckel, and Wilhelm Frick, and spent several hours a day speaking to Hermann Goering *ad hoc* before the trial began.[446] He went on to make a career with the Department of Defense.[447] Edward Hans Littman, formerly of the 3rd MRB company, also served as an interpreter at Nuremberg, then returned to Texas, where he pursued a career in law, filing restitution claims on behalf of clients who had survived occupation and internment in Germany, Poland, and Italy.[448]

Arthur Hadley became a war correspondent and served as a consultant on arms control and army training. Arthur Jaffe went to study at the Hebrew University in Jerusalem and served in Israeli military intelligence for three-and-a-half years before returning to make a distinguished career in the United States and to pursue a life-long passion

---

[445] Max W. Kraus, *They All Come to Geneva and Other Tales of a Public Diplomat*, 8.
[446] Interview of Gunter Kosse by Hans R. Weinmann, 22 July, 2011.
[447] Author interview with Gunter Kosse, 23 Sept. 2013.
[448] Littman's restitution case files are now housed at the Leo Baeck Institute in New York City.

for book art.

Albert Rosenberg got an advanced degree in community organization. He became involved trying to quell race issues in Baltimore, Chicago, Dayton, Detroit, and New Orleans, and worked in President Johnson's "war on poverty" program in five Ohio counties, before settling into an academic career in El Paso, Texas. He considers the five years he spent as cultural therapist for Hospice "the most important work I've ever done."[449]

After completing his studies at Bowling Green State University, Otto Schoeppler became chairman of two subsidiaries of Chase Manhattan Bank in London and Hong Kong. Fred Perutz became a director of the New York Cotton Exchange; Si Lewen became a renowned artist.

Igor Cassini wrote the "Cholly Knickerbocker" gossip columns and hosted two television shows; he married four times and maintained residences in his later years in Spain and Italy.

Walter Kohner found his fiancée in Amsterdam; they married in Luxembourg and, upon their return to the States, settled in Hollywood, where Walter worked as a Hollywood agent. In May 1953 Hanna Bloch Kohner was featured on Ralph Edwards' television broadcast *This is Your Life*. This was the first time that the story of a Holocaust survivor had been featured in the United States on national television. Later in life the two collaborated on the book *Hanna and Walter, A Love Story*.

"Ace" Seemann returned to the Camp Sharpe area to spend his life in his wife's hometown of Biglerville, Pennsylvania, while Gaston Pender and his wife moved to his former hometown in North Carolina.

Bert Anger became a business executive and was in charge of production and sales for factories in six European countries. Benno Frank became a distinguished theater director at an inter-racial theater in Cleveland and in Atlanta before moving permanently to Israel.

Philip Pines became a history teacher in New York; Heinz Deku remained in Germany and taught at the Ludwig-Maximilians University in Munich.

Edward Alexander, Arthur Bardos, and Max Kraus pursued careers in the U. S. Foreign Service. Alexander organized and recruited personnel for the Transcaucasian Branch of the *Voice of America* and initi-

---

[449] Albert Rosenberg interview with Sylvia Cohen, Tape 6.

ated broadcasts to the Soviet Union in Armenian, Azeri, Uzbek and Tatar. His tours of duty took him to Budapest, Athens, Berlin, and the Soviet bloc countries. Bardos served as public diplomacy Foreign Service Officer in American embassies in Vietnam, Guinea, Morocco, France, Belgium, Germany and Turkey. Kraus joined the U.S. Information Administration and held posts in Africa and the Far East; he served as a U.S. spokesman at the Vietnamese peace talks in Paris and SALT II meetings in Geneva, Switzerland.

Peter Wyden returned to the States to make a career as a writer and journalist. Several of the "Psycho Boys" returned to their pre-war jobs—Gaston Pender to his job as top salesman for General Mills, Eddie Amicone to his job as deliveryman for Railway Express in Youngstown, Ohio. Tony Strobl returned to his work as Disney artist in Hollywood, and Ernst Wynder to the research lab, to continue his investigations into the causes of lung cancer. Hans Deppisch returned to his old job as an insurance salesman in New York State. Clyde Shives became a leading figure in the plumbing industry and served as President of the American Foundry in Los Angeles.

Many, like Kosse, Wynder, Schoeppler, Rosenberg, Anger, Pines, and Samson Knoll took advantage of the GI bill to further their education. A goodly number of Sharpe men became university professors and administrators: Leon Edel at Princeton, New York University, and the University of Hawaii, Boris Kremenliev at UCLA, Milton Stern at UC/Berkeley, Albert Guerard at Stanford University, Oskar Seidlin at The Ohio State University and Indiana University, Joseph Eaton at the University of Pittsburgh, Samson Knoll at the Monterey Institute of Foreign Studies.

Some of the Sharpe men returned to live in Europe. Those with obvious communist leanings, such as Stefan Heym and Hanuš Burger, left in protest of America's Cold War policies; Stefan Heym even returned his bronze star in protest of America's entry into the Korean War. Heym settled in East Germany, where, for a time, he became a star propagandist for the Communist regime. After the fall of the Berlin Wall, he was elected to office in a reunited Germany as an independent Socialist. Hanuš Burger returned to Czechoslovakia, where he pursued his film-making until the 1968 Soviet repressions caused him to flee to Munich. There he continued working for film and television until his death.

Hans Habe, who was liberal rather than socialist or communist, also moved back to Europe. He settled in Switzerland, where he continued his career as a prolific writer of works of fiction and nonfiction, many of them critical of U.S. policy. He also acquired three more wives. Others left the United States for professional reasons. Fred Lorenz went back to his German name—Manfred Inger—and returned to the Vienna stage; Joseph Wechsberg also moved to Vienna, where he served as European correspondent for *The New Yorker*. Otto Schoeppler was enchanted with Switzerland during a visit he made there on his last furlough as an American soldier; he returned to make his permanent home there.

Many of the Sharpe men wrote memoirs about their training and service in the war, and at least five wrote novels about their war-time and immediate-postwar experiences—Hans Habe, whose novels focus on the American occupation of Germany (*Aftermath*, *Off Limits*, *Walk in Darkness*), Albert Guerard (*Night Journey*, an allegorical novel about the disillusionment of a young and idealistic military intelligence officer), Stefan Heym (*The Crusaders*, a long and ambitious roman à clef about Heym's MRB experiences during the war), Hanuš Burger (*1212 sendet.: Tatsachenroman* [1212 Is Broadcasting: a Factual Novel], about Operation "Annie") and Si Lewen (*Chronicle from Witzburg*, an examination into the mind of a concentration camp commander).

Many of the MRB men have returned to Gettysburg to see again the place where they trained for their European tour. A number of Sharpe men have arranged reunions with comrades from their MRB companies, most recently in 2011. Their bond is one that transcends party politics. In 2000, Stefan Heym spoke with Marco Martin, a reporter who mentioned that he wrote for the same conservative newspaper as Ernst Cramer. Heym responded: "Right, he works there as well, an *anti-Communist*. Sergeant Cramer and Sergeant Heym—two young Jews who had barely escaped the Nazis a life-time ago, and trained in America's Camp Sharpe for the landing in Normandy. Not that we particularly liked each other—but please give my greetings to him, won't you?" Martin noted that "suddenly—one year before he died—the old man's eyes filled with tears."[450] For Heym, for Cramer, Camp Sharpe had been a gathering place for "good" Germans, who united there with Americans and with anti-Fascists from the other European countries in order to train for a specialized war against the barbarity of Hitler's Germany. Forty years after his service at Camp Sharpe Heym noted, "The ideas of Gettysburg have had an influence on my thinking up to this day—that speech of Lincoln's has never lost

---

[450] Marko Martin, "Sie schreiben für diese Springerpresse, was?," *Die Welt*, 10 Apr. 2013.

its meaning."[451] When he was well into his nineties, Cramer expressed the same thought, saying, "Even though democracy had its roots in Europe, I learned practical democracy, 'government of the people, by the people, for the people,' in America."[452] As "paragraphtroopers"[453] who chose words over rifles as their weaponry of choice, the men from Sharpe had fought to preserve ideals rather than to extinguish lives. Small wonder, then, that the muddy grounds of Gettysburg retained for many of them a lingering, if faint, utopian luster.

---

[451] Letter from Stefan Heym to Arthur W. McCardle, 19 July 1984.
[452] Ernst Cramer, "Standing Together—Opening remarks by Professor Ernst Cramer at the 59th Convention."
[453] [Clyde Shives] *5th Mobile Radio Broadcasting Company.*

Appendix

Members of the MRB Companies that Trained in Gettysburg

Most of the names that are listed here were given to me by Daniel Gross, who is conducting a much larger study of Maryland's Camp Ritchie and the men who trained there. This list is not guaranteed to be a complete one, since not all the men who were sent to Camp Sharpe passed though training at Camp Ritchie. Commissioned officers, where known, are indicated with an asterisk; I have included, in parentheses, alternate and middle names that some soldiers used instead of their given first names, as well as original names used prior to military service. I have put in brackets names some soldiers adopted when no longer in the military service; in a few cases I note, with both parentheses and brackets, that a soldier reverted to his original name after the war. There was a great deal of movement in assignment between the various MRB companies. I have tried, wherever possible, to put these men into the last known company in which they served, but also to indicate the other MRB companies to which they were assigned at some point in their service. I do not include assignments to another body, such as *Stars and Stripes*, OSS, or OWI, nor do I include the names of civilians assigned to the MRB companies, since they did not have military training in Gettysburg. It is possible that a few of the soldiers listed here did not train at Camp Sharpe but were transferred into these companies after they were already in the European theater. I accept responsibility for any errors of listing.

Camp Sharpe Commandant: John T. Jarecki
Camp Sharpe Instructor: Hans Habe (Janos Békessy)

SECOND MOBILE RADIO BROADCASTING COMPANY

Commanding Officers

*Maxwell Grabove
*Arthur H. Jaffe

Company Members

A
Leo T. Abati
Eddie Eugene Amicone
William V. Anderson
Bert Walther Anger
Michael G. Arab
R. E. Arnhold
Nicholas Samuel Ayoub

B
Joseph S. Baltuch
Anthony F. Baranowski {also 3rd MRB}
Peter Barbieri
Edward W. Bardgett, Jr.
Albrecht P. Barsis {also 3rd MRB}
Edward A. Beach
Russell E. Beckwith
Ulis S. Beeler, Jr.
Thomas J. Benkosky
J. C. Bennett
Earl E. Bensen {also 3rd MRB}
*Robert G. (Glenn) Bernbaum
Jean Pierre Best
Alfred Biagi
John A. Billy {also 3rd MRB}
*William P. Bird {also 3rd MRB}
Charles Biro, Jr.
Lothar Bloch {also 3rd MRB}
Victor Bonic
*Russell J. Bowen
Otto Brand
Forrest Thomas Brewster

Byron R. Buck
Hans Herbert (Hanuš) Burger

C
Saverio Caltagirone
Rene E. Chauvin {also 4th MRB}
Michael Rocco Cirino
Robert E. Click
Kenneth B. Coleman {also 3rd MRB}
John Collier
Anthony N. Colosimo
Rudy Cook (Rudolph Cluk)
Peter Copulos, Jr.
Richard W. Corduan

D
Carlo J. Degioanni
Heinz (Henry) Deku (Heinz Dekuczynski)
Hans Curt Deppisch
Olcott R. Dole
Joseph S. Dominick, Jr.
Keith F. Downing
Leon Adolphe Dreyfus [Leon Andrew Dale]

E
Carl Elson (orig. Elyovic)
William H. Elson, Jr.
Gustaf A. Espling {also 3rd MRB}

F

Sylvester Fanti
Frederick F. Feibel
Joseph Feldstein
William Fischer
Robert Foraste
Alessandro (Alexander) Frank
Benno D. Frank
*Gordon M. Frick

G

Benjamin Gibbons
Deforest W. Goodrum
Homer Graf
George Grossman
Albert Joseph Guerard
Nolan J. Guillory

H

George Alfred Hahn {also 4th MRB}
Charles C. Haines
Ero John Heino {also 3rd MRB}
Isador Henig
David Herber {also 3rd MRB}
Stefan Heym (Helmut Flieg)
Richard J. Higgins
Harry A. Hoffman
*George R. Holbert
Albert P. Houde
Jesse Louis Howerton
Talmadge E. Huey

I

Henry E. Interdonato
Christopher E. Inzinga {also 3rd MRB}

J

Albert E. Jeannotte
Curt Jellin (Jelinofski)

Henry A. Johnston, Jr.
Herbert J. Johnston

K

Jack Katz
Konrad Kellen (Katzenellenbogen)
Paul E. Kelley
Elmer F. Klementis
John Klosowski
Samson B. Knoll
Henri Kops
Peter Kosminsky {also 3rd MRB}
Boris A. Kremenliev {also 4th MRB}
Harry A. Krueger

L

Gunther Lanson (Lichtenstein)
*Jean S. LaRue {also 3rd MRB}
Urho W. Latva
Richard Le Grelle
Emil Lehman (Sprinzeles)
Frank J. Leonard
Arthur Levy
*Charles A. Lifschultz
Stephan M. Lisiecki
William Locke
*Charles Lowenthal

M

James O. McCarry
Lyle A. McManus
Ludwig Mahler
Carl D. Malone
*Richard E. Mann
John Manoush
Lawrence E. Martin
Bruno M. Massimi
Kaudo B. Maison
Sam D. Mauro

Leon Medeiros
Gordon R. Melgren
Louis M. Mellitz
Fred Messinger
Thomas E. Metcalf
Wendall H. Metcalf
*Irving B. Mickey
*Elmer R. Mosher
Rudolf Moskovits
*Louis C. Muhlbauer
William H. Myers

N
Anthony R. Nagy
August Narduzzi, Jr.
Walter C. North

O
*Daniel Overton

P
Matthew L. Paluszek
Philip S. Passuello
Chester P. Pagtrick
Harold U. Peddicord
*Willie E. Petty
Sarkis Phillian
Arthur W. Picard
Philip Pinkofsky [Pines]
Fred Placek
Joseph Frank Poerio
Leon E. Poussard {also 3rd MRB}
John Sam Puglisi

R
Herman M. Raabe
Walter M. Reichenbach
George L. Riffe
Ernest R. Rodriguez
*Eugene A. Rotterman, Jr. {3rd MRB}

*James W. Rugg
Michael Rusinol

S
William J. Sailer
*Albert H. Salvatori
Ernest Sancho-Bonet
Urbano Sbrocca {also 3rd MRB}
Rudolf Schattner
Wilmer C. Schmidt {also 4th MRB}
Otto Schoeppler, Jr.
*Francis Seidler {also 3rd MRB}
Oskar Seidlin (Oskar Koplowitz) {also 3rd MRB}
James H. Seifert {also 3rd MRB}
Eugene J. Seitz
Erik Simonson
Philip A. Siragusa {also 3rd MRB}
Frank L. Smith
Joseph F. Sonowski
Steve Spaich {also 3rd MRB}
Arthur L. St. Sauveur
Henry E. Stanton
Emanuel D. Starer
Gino E. Stefano
Walter Straus

T
Parks T. Taylor
Harry Teitelbaum
*Jacob I. Tennenbaum
Arthur C. Tetreault, Jr.
Henry E. Thomforde [Henry J. Thomforde]
John Tola
Emil J. Tullio

V
Enno Vanderveen, Jr.
Frank W. Vetock

*Arthur C. Vogel {also 3rd MRB}

W

George Fuller Walker II
Sylvester E. Wallock {also 3rd MRB}
Russel Warren
Peter H. Weidenreich [Wyden]
*Morris Wigler
William Wilkow
Leonard N. Willig
Martin V. Wilson
Raymond G. Wilson
Laurence J. Wingate {also 5th MRB?}
Theodore Woehl
Charles Lenard Wurts

Z

Willard L. Zimmerman
John A. Zincio

THIRD MOBILE RADIO BROADCASTING COMPANY

Commanding Officer

*John E. Paulson

Company Members

A

Kurt S. Adler
Herman Alexander
Arsenio Alfaro
Milton Amgott

B

Joseph Baer
*Harry L. Baker
Jules M. Baron
George F. Barry
John J. Bauer
*Rudolf Baum
Robert Beck
Wilfred G. Behrend {also 2nd MRB}
Albert J. Bekaert {also 2nd MRB}
Erwin Benkow {also 2nd MRB}
Earl E. Bensen {also 2nd MRB}
Gary C. Bernier
Arturo C. Berriochoa
Emanuel Bocra

*Jules Jerome Bond (Bondy)
Harry R. Boyd {also 4th MRB}
Andrew Harold Brenick
Rudolph F. Brooks
Byron R. Buck {also 2nd MRB}

C

Jack A. Caminer (Hans Wolfgang Caminer)
Johnie B. Carraway
Montero J. Casci
Fabio Coen {also 1st MRB}
John Alan Coffman
*Jack Travis Collette
Eugene Cooney
Jose T. Coss
Armand J. Cossette
Ernest (Ernst) J. Cramer {also 2nd MRB}
Louis T. Cronenberger
Shakeeb Saleh Dakour

D
Mike D'Annunzio
Henry Darmstadter
Frederick N. DeBell
Angelo DeFazio
Antonio (Anthony) Di Matteo
Paul Dimech

E
Joseph (Leon) Edel
Paul A. Eisler {also 2nd MRB}
Sherman Erickson
Earl S. Ettinger

F
Douglas G. Fish {also 2nd MRB}
Nathaniel Friedman
Paul J. Friedman
*Raymond L. Fuller {also 2nd MRB}

G
Biagio Gagilardi
Thomas A. Gardner
John P. Gaydosh
Robert T. Gill {also 2nd MRB}
Forrest R. Gowen

H
Clifton D. Hall
Georg(e) Wolfgang Felix Hallgarten {also 2nd MRB}
*Homer C. Hansen
Frank A. Harasick {also 2nd MRB}
Henry R. Hauger
Ole Haugland (Ingolf H. Clarke)
Walter L. Henschel
Eric Hertz {also 2nd MRB}
Gottfried Hesse
*Charles H. Hoffman

Michael Holowascko Jr.
William F. Huber
Michael Hudak

J
Richard E. Johansson {also 2nd MRB}
Herbert J. Johnston {also 2nd MRB}

K
Walter Anthony Klinger
Nils T. Knagenhjelm {also 2nd MRB}
Boris Krass
Kaare Kvale

L
Thomas G. Lanzetta
Nicholas J. Laurens {also 2nd MRB}
Arthur B. Laurie
Paul W. Layden
Alfred S. Leiman
*Leonard A. Lemlein
Charles E. Leveille
Simon J. Lewin [Si Lewen] {also 2nd MRB}
Nicholas Lijoi
Joseph L. Liop {also 4th MRB}
*Edward Hans Littman {also 2nd MRB}
Herbert Lobl {also 2nd MRB}
Karl J. Loewenstein
John Joseph Lombardi
Henry W. Longley {also 5th MRB}
Fred Lorenz [(Manfred Inger)] {also 2nd MRB}
Geoffrey Louth {also 4th MRB}

M
Abraham Mandelberg
Raylite J. Marshall
Egidio Mauro
Sam Donato Mauro
George W. McGill {also 2nd MRB}
Milton F. Meinke
Thomas F. Middleton Jr.
Harry R. Moretti
Charles E. Mulligan
*Alfred F. Munzel

N
Guy R. Nichols
Nils C. Nilson
Walter C. North
Rudolf S. Nothmann

P
William B. Pfeiffer
Bruno Ponzi
Carl Victor Princi {also 2nd MRB}

R
Edward R. Rebich {also 4th MRB}
John Allen Reed {also 2nd MRB}
John H. Remak
Emerson R. Rich
Robert H. Roberts
Peter A. Robertson
Gerard Rohde
Leo J. Roy

S
Alex Zoltan Sagi
Joseph Salvino
James Saulnier
Wilfred C. (Bill) Schoenberg
Alan L. Schweiger
Albert F. Scribner
Horace R. Seaback
*Clarence L. ("Ace") Seemann
Theodor Siesel
Henry Sievers
Everett J. Steiger {also 2nd MRB}
William Henry Stevens {also 2nd MRB}
Anthony J. (Tony) Strobl, Jr.

T
Peter A. Todoroff
James E. Tracy {also 2nd MRB}

U
Richard F. Ury {also 2nd MRB}

V
Henry H. J. Van Der Voort {also 2nd MRB}
Alio Vanni
Milo Vujnovich

W
Stanley J. Wielechowski {also 2nd MRB}
Kurt Wittler
Theodore Woehl
Friedrich Wolinsky {also 2nd MRB}
William V. Wortkoetter

Z
Edmund B. Zadok {also 2nd MRB}

Fourth Mobile Radio Broadcasting Company

Commanding Officer
*Joseph C. Goularte

Company Members

A
Robert L. Addis
Hans Adler {also 2nd MRB}
Alfred Agins
Eugene Aguirre {also 2nd MRB}
Richard Akselrad
Harry E. Alley
Henry C. Alter
Kurt R. Andreas
Sol Applebaum
Theodore Arlt

B
Alexander Babin
Gary Babin
Arthur Alexander Bardos
Simon Barendse
Richard Barnes
Frederick K. (Edward) Bauer
*Alexandre Behr
William H. Bell, Jr.
Hyman Berger
Trygve Berghorn
Emil L. Beseau
Ernest S. Biberfield
Otis Bishop
Manfred Blatner
Erling H. Boggild
Fred G. Bopp
Paul Joachim Brand
Willard H. Bredenberg
Roger C. Brett
Robert Breuer
Gabriel Bossio Bruno

Raynold F. Budden

C
John J. Cassese
Jose de Chimay
Edward Cooper Clarenbach {also 3rd MRB}
Harley Cook
C. S. Cordova
Diego C. Costanzo {also 3rd MRB}
Paul K. Cunningham, Jr.

D
Louis J. De Milhau {also 5th MRB}
Thomas Dennis [(orig. Tibor de Scitovsky)]
Richard A. De Santis
*—Devilbiss
Libero Di Via
Paul Dimech
Zygmunt Dolinski
Bernard C. Dullea

E
*Edward D. Easton
Joseph W. Eaton (Josef Wechsler)
Zaky Eldin
Charles Englebert de Fernelmont
David Epstein

F
Leo D. Fialkoff

G
Edward Geers
James D. Gilstrom
Charles H. Girt
Maurice H. Greenberger
Paul F. Guenther

H
Kenneth R. Harrari
*Mark Henry Hermer
Kenneth C. Hoag
Michael J. Holubz
Joseph F. Horvath {also 3rd MRB}
Roy C. Huelsenkamp {also 2nd MRB}

J
Charles R. Jacobson
Gerald C. Johnston {also 2nd MRB}
Michael Josselson

K
Samuel George Kaleel {also 2nd MRB?}
William G. Kammerer
Norris A. Kaprielian
George V. Karis
Anthony J. Kida
Max M. Kimenthal
Jacob Koffler {also 2nd MRB}
Walter Kohner
Hanns H. Kolmar
Robert Korn {also 2nd MRB}

L
Victor Lamerlis

Norton R. Laurie
Armando G. Le Clerc {also 3rd MRB}
Wilfred Leger
*Willard Levy {also 5th MRB}
Ernest H. Loewenbein {also 3rd MRB}
Max Logan (Loeffel)
John S. Lugt
Michael Joseph Lyons

M
Leonard J. Marrone
Lemuel Paul Marvel
Ralph T. Mastoloni
Felix Mayer {also 2nd MRB}
Helmut Mayer
Paul A. Mayer
John Mayernick Jr.
Ernest Mehlman
Adolph E. Meier
James I. Merkel
O'Leamon Merritt
Louis J. de Milhau
Joseph Julius Miller
George F. Muller {also 5th MRB}

O
Albert F. Orbaan

P
Marius Pedersen
*Gaston Lewis Pender
Francis D. Perkins
John H. Perkins
James J. Perry
Fred W. Perutz
Stanley A. Pigulski

R
Herbert Irvine Raney

Edward I. Rauma
George P. Raymond {also 2nd MRB}
Bernhard H. Reijmers {also 5th MRB}
Jack Reingold
Earnest E. Revell
*A. Ristow
Steven J. Roes
*Albert G. Rosenberg
Francis Joseph Ross
Stevens J. Ross

S

Harry Sachs {also 2nd and 5th MRB}
Alfred H. Sampson
Aurelio Sandoval
Thomas Sardina
Herbert Schlesinger
Julius Schreiber
Sam Sciurba {also 2nd MRB}
Gerald Shall
Andrew Slavik (Slavick)
Anthony M. Stefano {also 2nd MRB}
Milton Reid Stern
Donald A. Sutherland

T

Joseph Thalhammer
Elmo J. Theriault

Dale A. Thomas
Lloyd Teify Thomas
Leonard Tremblay

U

Robert M. Uhl

V

John A. Vallindras

W

Joseph Wechsberg
George Wegener
S. Weisenfeld
Ignatz Wild
Earl B. Wilson
William M. Windsor {also 2nd MRB}

Y

Edward J. Yeager

Z

George E. Zachariades {also 2nd MRB}
Gabriel Zakin
Paul G. Zeleny
Harrison (Harry) Arthur Zeplin
Gus Ziegler
Ewald Ziffer

Fifth Mobile Radio Broadcasting Company

Commanding Officer
*Robert Asti

Company Members

A

Franklin M. Adams
George S. Alberts
Edward Alexander {also 4th MRB}
Albert A. Alverson, Sr.
Ernest S. Anderen
Norman A. Askeland {also 3rd MRB}
Louis Atlas {also 3rd and 4th MRB}

B

William G. Baksa
Charles L. Barber
Charles E. Bard
John P. Barricelli
*Alfred W. Bass
Herbert F. Bender
Theodore Beresovski
David Berger {also 4th MRB}
Lloyd Bickford
Harold R. Bland
Robert M. Boyer
Albert A. Brown
Adolph G. Buettner

C

Andrew V. Cangelosi
Francis J. Canning
Sidney Captain
Edward G. Carter
Michael M. Casiero

Igor Cassini {also 3rd and 4th MRB}
Carl L. Chase
Philip P. Chiavaras
Ralph Collier
James F. Corson {also 4th MRB}
Floyd F. Crowell

D

John F. Diener
Elmer Dolqueist
William Hubert Duncan

E

Helmuth Eckhardt
Daniel J. Edelman {also 4th MRB}
Kurt H. Ehlers {also 4th MRB}
Walter Ehrenberger
*Hans J. Epstein

F

Charles W. Fairbanks
Guerino John Fanelli
James V. Favata, Jr.
Samuel P. Faynor
Frederick E. Finger
Anthony Forlenza
Charles P. France
Roderick H. Fruendt
Frederick W. Furtick

G

Hans Wilhelm Gatzke
*Karl S. Gerlt

Walter C. Glass {also 3rd and 4th MRB}
Frank J. Grasso
Carl K. Greenberg
Hans P. Greenwood
*Jon M. Groetzinger {also 2nd and 3rd MRB}
John A. Gruber {also 2nd and 3rd MRB}

H

*Arthur T. Hadley
Frank S. Halcarz
George Hale
Tage B. Hansen
Stanley E. Harris
*Peter H. Hart {also 4th MRB}
George R. Hartikainen
*Ira J. Harvey
Esko A. Hautamaki
Levi H. Heidrich
William O. Heissner
Gerard G. Hilston {also 4th MRB}
Claude Edward Himmelberger
David L. Hinkin
Fred C. Hinrichs
*William T. Hudgins

J

Henry R. Jacobson
Harold M. Jaffe
Richard E. Johannsson
Nils Johnson

K

Siegmund Kauffmann
Peter Kocsi {also 4th MRB}
Max Kraus {also 4th MRB}
Wilho Kyllonen

L

Roger A. Lajoie
Abram V. (Victor) Lasky {also 4th MRB}
*Dayton F. Latham
Rene R. Lauzier
Vincent Y. Le Crann
Robert S. Leeds
Werner Lehnberg
John Leholm
Owen A. Lehr
Nicholas Lenovits
Donald D. Leonard {also 2nd MRB}
David J. Levy
*Jerome J. Lewin
George Lewis
Merton J. Lonn
James H. Lowe

M

Herbert Mahler
Leo Marcoux
Jack March
Howard K. Marr
Chester C. McVey
*Rod F. Meaney
Abram Medow
Christian W. Meyer
Anthony N. Mirco
Louis F. Mora
Alfred E. Mueller
Frank E. Murphy

N

Richard Niess

P

Clark L. Patriquin
Alfred M. Petersen
William A. Plice

Ernest M. Plozner

R

Leon Racine {also 4th MRB}
Herbert Irvine Raney {also 3rd and 4th MRB}
Emanuel Rapoport
Peter E. Razukas
Henri R. Reiman
Raymond B. Remillard
William H. Rieser
Edward J. Ross {also 4th MRB}
George R. Rowen {also 4th MRB}
Leopold P. Ruff {also 4th MRB}
Veryl W. Rupp

S

Harry Sachs
William B. Scheulen
Bernard (Bernd) G. Schlesinger
*Frederick C. Schnurr, Jr.
William Schreier {also 2nd and 4th MRB}
Harry E. Schultz
Felix C. Schurich
Harold (Hal) Rossman Seymour
Wilbur J. Sheehan
Clyde E. Shives
Alex E. Shotland
Walter M. Simon
Edward D. Spear
Gerard W. Speyer
Marvin A. Stiely
Paul W. Stiely

Joseph E. Stranzl
Irvin Y. Straus
William J. Sullivan

T

Harold Tager, Jr. {also 4th MRB}
Irving S. Taubkin {also 4th MRB}
Paul J. Tew
Erwin H. Tietjen
George Tobias
Abe H. Truskinoff
Francis P. Tunney

U

John H. Ubben {also 4th MRB}
Richard W. Uhlig

V

Adolph Van Hollander
Fred W. Van Hoorn
August R. Vavrus
Victor A. Velen

W

Conrad A. Waltmann
Alphonse F. Weil {also 4th MRB}
Edgar K. Welch
Charles Weston
Michael P. Williams
Charles Z. Wilson
Eric(h) Winters {also 4th MRB}
Ernest (Ernst) L. Wynder

Bibliography

Interviews and Correspondence

Alexander, Edward. Interview with author. 21 June 2013.
Amicone, Eddie E. Letter to author. November 22, 2013.
Bardos, Arthur A. Interview with Hans Tuch, *The Association for Diplomatic Studies and Training, Foreign Affairs Oral History Project*, 25 Jan. 1990.
>http://www.adst.org/OH%20TOCs/Bardos,%20Arthur%20A,toc.pdf

Bernsdorff, Walter and Martin Vialon, "Vom Um-Erzieher zum Freund: Interview mit Samson B. Knoll—Offizier der amerikanischen Militärregierung in Marburg." In: Benno Hafeneger and Wolfram Schäfer, eds. *Aufbruch zwischen Mangel und Verweigerung, Marburg in den Nachkriegsjahren 2.* Marburg: Rathaus-Verlag, 2000, 21-44.
Eaton, Joseph. Interview with Judith Cohen, United States Holocaust Memorial Museum. 1 Aug. 2010.
>http://collections.ushmm.org/search/catalog/irn41725

Jacobs, Harry. Interview with author. 2 Oct. 2013.
Jaffe, Arthur H. Interviews with author. 11 July, 1 Aug., 29 Dec. 2013.
Jellin, Curt. Interview with Rosalyn Manowitz, Dec. 9, 1977. Presented to the United States Holocaust Memorial Museum, 13 Oct. 1993.
>http://collections.ushmm.org/search/catalog/irn510624

Kosse, Gunter. Interviews with author. 23 Sept., 9 Oct. 2013, 18 Jan. 2014.
—. Interview with Hans R. Weinmann. 22 July 2011.
>http://www.holocaustcenter.org/page.aspx?pid=801

Kraus, Max W. Interview with Cliff Groce. Initial interview date 1988. *The Association for Diplomatic Studies and Training, Foreign Affairs Oral History Project, Information Series.* Copyright 1998 by the ADST.
Lewen, Si. Interview with author. 26 July 2013.
Perutz, Fred W. Interviews with author. 28 Sept., 1, 13 Oct. 2013.

Pines, Philip, Interview with author. 15 Aug. 2013; letter of 22 Oct. 2013.
Rosenberg, Albert G. Interview with Sylvia Cohen, 10 Aug. 1998, in El Paso TX. Interview code 43931. *Visual History Archive*. USC Shoah Foundation. Web. 4 Apr. 2014.
—. Interviews with author. 6, 13 Jan. 2014.
Schoeppler, Otto. Letters to author, 18 Aug., 2 Sept., 23 Oct. 2013.
Stern, Milton R. Interview with Ann Lage, 1992. In Milton R. Stern, "The Learning Society: Continuing Education at NYU, Michigan, and UC Berkeley, 1946-1991," Regional Oral History Office, The Bancroft Library, University of California, Berkeley, 1993.

Books and Articles

Anderton, Abby: "'It was Never a Nazi Orchestra': The American Re-education of the Berlin Philharmonic." *Music & Politics* VII:1 (Winter 2013).
    http://dx.doi.org/10.3998/mp.9460447.0007.103
Anger, Bert W. "From Hanover to the Elbe." In Leo F. Caproni, Jr. and Joanna S. Caproni, eds. *Dartmouth at War*. Dartmouth Class of 1942, 2011, 8-13.
"Around the Jewish World: Germany's Past and Future Reflected in Honor for German Jewish Journalist," *JTA, The Global Jewish News Source*, 17 Oct. 2003.
    http://www.jta.org/2003/10/17/archive/around-the-jewish-world-germanys-past-and-future-reflected-in-honor-for-german-jewish-journalist
Atkinson, Rick. *The Guns at Last Light: The War in Western Europe, 1944-1945*. New York: Henry Holt and Company, 2013.
Bauer, Christian and Rebekka Göpfert. *Die Ritchie Boys: Deutsche Emigranten beim US-Geheimdienst*. Hamburg: Hoffmann und Campe, 2005.
Bernauer, James, "The Holocaust and the Catholic Church's Search for Forgiveness." A Presentation at Boston College's Center for Religion and American Public Life, 30 Oct. 2002.
    www.bc.edu/research/cjl/metaelements/texts/cjrelations/resources/articles/benauer.htm
"Bitterer Lorbeer." *Der Spiegel*, 30 Sept. 1953, 14-15.
Black, Robert W. *Rangers in World War II*. NY: Ivy Books, 1992.
Boyce, Michael. *Tyntesfield in WWII*. Bristol (U.K.): SilverWood Books, 2012.

Brokaw, Tom. *An Album of Memories: Personal Histories from the Greatest Generation.* New York: Random House, 2001.

Burger, H. H. [Hanuš]. "Operation Annie: Now It Can Be Told." *New York Times Magazine.* 17 Feb. 1946, 12-13, 48, 50.

Burger, Hanuš. *1212 sendet.. Tatsachenroman.* Berlin: Deutscher Militärverlag, 1965.

—. "Episode on the Western Front." *New York Times Magazine,* 26 Nov. 1944, 5, 52.

—. *Der Frühling war es wert. Erinnerungen.* Munich: C. Bertelsman, 1977.

Edward A. Caskey, "Introduction," *PWB Combat Team...,* [Washington, D.C., 1944]

Cassini, Igor. *I'd do it all over again.* New York: G. P. Putnam's Sons, 1977.

Craft, Ray K. *Psychological Warfare in the European Theater of Operation,* Study Number 131, [1945].

Cramer, Ernst. "Address for the Convocation of a Memorial Tablet for the Jewish Victims of Nazism from Augsburg." Delivered in the Golden Hall of the Augsburg City Hall on July 9, 2001.
http://www.infotrue.com/mempro.html

—."Standing Together—Opening remarks by Professor Ernst Cramer at the 59th Convention." Verband der Deutsch-Amerikanischen Clubs.
http://www.vdac.de/vdac/index.php?option=com_content&task=view&id=192&Itemid=143&lang=en

—. "Worst Disaster in German History. Have we learned the lesson of Auschwitz?" *The Atlantic Times. A Monthly Newspaper from Germany,* Feb. 2005.
http://www.atlantic-times.com/archive_detail.php?recordID=111

Daugherty, William E. *A Psychological Warfare Casebook.* Baltimore: The Johns Hopkins Press, 1960 [1958].

"Defenders of Luxembourg," *Broadcasting,* 16 Apr. 1945, 23.

Leon Edel, *The Visitable Past: A Wartime Memoir.* Honolulu: University of Hawai'i, 2000.

"Former Local Officer Tells of War Action." *The Gettysburg Times,* 19 Feb. 1945.

Fox, Elise Scharf. *Hotel Gettysburg, A Landmark In Our Nation's History.* Ed. Harry Stokes. Gettysburg: Downtown Gettysburg, 1988.

Frank, Benno. "No Bread and Circuses for Germany." OMGUS, *Information Bulletin* 30 (23 Feb. 1946), 5-8.

Friedman, Herbert A. and Franklin Prosser. "The United States PSYOP Organization in Europe During World War II." http://www.psywarrior.com/PSYOPOrgWW2.html

Gienow-Hecht, Jessica C. E. *Transmission Impossible: American Journalism as Cultural Diplomacy in Postwar Germany 1945-1955*. Baton Rouge: Louisiana State University, 1999.

Guerard, Albert J. *Night Journey*. New York: Alfred A. Knopf, 1950.

—. *The Touch of Time: Myth, Memory and the Self*. Stanford CA: Stanford Alumni Association, 1980.

Habe, Hans. *Aftermath. A Novel*. Tr. Richard F. Hanser. New York: The Viking Press, 1947.

—. *All My Sins. An Autobiography*. Tr. E. Osers, London, Toronto Wellington, Sydney: George G. Harrap & Co., 1957.

—. *Off Limits: A Novel*. Tr. Ewald Osers,. London: George G. Harrap, 1956.

—. *Walk in Darkness*. Tr. Richard Hanser. New York: G. P. Putnam's Sons, 1948.

Hackett, David A, tr. ed. *The Buchenwald Report*. Boulder, San Francisco, Oxford: Westview Press, 1995.

Hadley, Arthur T. "Firing Potent Words, From a Tank." *New York Times*, 25 Sept. 2006.

—. *Heads or Tails: A Memoir*. New York: Glitterati, 2007.

—. "Is This Like Your War, Sir?" *The Atlantic Monthly*, September 1972.
http://www.theatlantic.com/past/docs/unbound/bookauth/battle/hadley.htm

—. "The 'Propaganda' Tank." In William E. Daugherty, *A Psychological Warfare Casebook*. Baltimore: The Johns Hopkins Press, 1960 [1958], 567-569.

"Here and There." *The Star and Sentinel* [Gettysburg], 15 July 1944.

Hertz, David. "The Radio Siege of Lorient." In William E. Daugherty, *A Psychological Warfare Casebook*. Baltimore: The Johns Hopkins Press, 1960 [1958], 384-392.

Heym, Stefan. *The Crusaders*. Boston: Little, Brown, 1948.

—. "I Am Only a Little Man." *New York Times Magazine*, 10 Sept. 1944, 9, 44-45.

—. *The Lenz Papers*, Berlin: Seven Seas Publishers, 1958.

—. *Nachruf*. Frankfurt/Main: Fischer Taschenbuch Verlag, 1994.

—. *Reden an den Feind*. Ed. Peter Mallwitz. Berlin: Verlag Neues Leben, 1986.

"Ich will nicht verdrängen!" *Bild*, 28 Jan. 2013.

http://www.bild.de/politik/inland/holocaust/ich-will-nicht-verdraengen-28278766.bild.html

Infoplease, http://www.infoplease.com/ipa/A0004598.html

Jacobson, Mark. *The Lampshade: A Holocaust Detective Story from Buchenwald to New Orleans*. New York, London, Toronto, Sydney: Simon & Schuster, 2010.

[Jaffe, Arthur H.]. *History, Second Mobile Radio Broadcasting Company, December 1943-May 1945.* n.p., n.d.

Jones, Syd. "Austrian Americans." *Countries and Their Cultures*. http://www.everyculture.com/multi/A-Br/Austrian-Americans.html#b#ixzz2ttiagzxf

Kellen, Konrad. *Katzenellenbogen: Erinnerungen an Deutschland*. Vienna: Edition Selene, c. 2003.

Kohner, Hanna and Walter, with Frederick Kohner. *Hanna and Walter: A Love Story*. New York: Random House, 1984.

Kraus, Max W. *They All Come to Geneva and Other Tales Of a Public Diplomat*. Cabin John, MD/Washington D.C.: Seven Locks Press, 1988.

Lehr, Owen A. "Ham Radio in Europe After V-J Day." *QCWA Journal*, Summer 1995, 46-47.

Lerner, Daniel. *Psychological Warfare against Nazi Germany: The Sykewar Campaign, D-Day to VE-Day*. Cambridge MA and London: The M.I.T. Press, 1971.

Levine, Alan J. *The Strategic Bombing of Germany, 1940-1945*. Westport CT: Praeger Publishers, 1992.

Lewen, Si. *Chronicle from Witzburg: A Novel*.
http://www.silewen.com/new/Chronicle%20From%20Witzburg.pdf

—. *Reflections and Repercussions: A Memoir*.
http://www.silewen.com/script/toc.html

"The liberation of Buchenwald at 3:15 p.m. on April 11, 1945."
http://www.furtherglory.wordpress.com

"Lieut. Collette Reburied Monday." *The Morning Herald*, Hagerstown Maryland, 19 Apr. 1949.

"Lt. Jack Collette Killed in Action." *The Daily Mail*, Hagerstown Maryland, 3 Apr. 1945.

Ljungström, Henrik. "Queen Elizabeth, 1940-1973."
http://www.thegreatoceanliners.com/queenelizabeth.html

M. J. [Morris Janowitz]. "William Joyce, Propagandist of Treason." In William E. Daugherty, *A Psychological Warfare Casebook*. Baltimore: The Johns Hopkins Press, 1960 [1958], 235-237.

Martin, Marko. "Sie schreiben für diese Springerpresse, was?" *Die Welt*, 10 Apr. 2013.
"Miss Howe and Officer Are Wed." *The Gettysburg Times*, 28 Apr. 1944.
Morgan, Brewster. "Operation Annie." *The Saturday Evening Post*, 9 Mar. 1946, 19, 121-124.
Prosser, Frank and SGM Herbert A. Friedman (Ret.), "Organization of the United States Propaganda Effort During World War II." http://www.psywar.co.uk/usa.php
"Radio: Operation Annie," *TIME Magazine*, 25 Feb. 1946.
Remy, Steven P. "Hans Habe, Stefan Heym and Guy Stern as 'Citizen Soldiers' and Cultural Mediators." In Fehervary, Helen and Bernd Fischer, eds. *Kulturpolitik und Politik der Kultur / Cultural Politics and Politics of Culture. Festschrift für Alexander Stephan / Essays to Honor Alexander Stephan*. Oxford, Bern, Berlin, et al: Peter Lang, 2007, 323-339.
Semprún, Jorge. *Literature or Life*. Tr. Linda Coverdale. New York: Penguin Books, 1998.
"'Service Wives' Club Is Planned." *The Gettysburg Times*, 19 Apr. 1944.
"Seven Service Wives in Club." *Gettysburg Star and Sentinel*, 6 May 1944.
[Shives, Clyde]. "History of the Fifth." *Fifth Mobile Radio Broadcasting Company*. n.p., n.d.
"Temporary Army Camp on 'Field.'" *Gettysburg Compiler*, 13 Nov. 1943.
[U.S. Army]. *PWB Combat Team...* [Washington, D.C., 1944].
W. E. D. [William E. Daugherty]. "Benno Frank, An American Propagandist." In William E. Daugherty, *A Psychological Warfare Casebook*. Baltimore: The Johns Hopkins Press, 1960 [1958], 248-251.
Wechsberg, Joseph. *Homecoming*. New York: Alfred A. Knopf, 1946.
Welsch, Eva-Juliane. *Die hessischen Lizenzträger und ihre Zeitungen*. Inauguraldissertation, Universität Dortmund, 2002. https://eldorado.tu-dortmund.de/bitstream/2003/2967/2/welschunt.pdf.txt
Wolf, Tom. "Novel 'Hog Calling' Offensive Crushes Morale of the Nazis." *Carroll Daily Times Herald* (Carroll, Iowa), 26 Aug. 1944.
Woolf, S. J. "Battle of Bulletins Frays Enemy Nerves." *Geneva Daily Times*," 11 July 1944.
Wyden, Peter. "Die bunte Truppe von Camp Shapiro." *Rheinischer Merkur* 18 (5 May 1995): 37.
—. *Stella*. New York, London, et al.: Simon & Schuster, 1992.

Zachau, Reinhard K. "'Gute Europäer in Amerikas Uniform': Hans Habe und Stefan Heym in der Psychological Warfare." In Helmut F. Pfanner, ed. *Der Zweite Weltkrieg und die Exilanten: Eine literarische Antwort*. Bonn: Bouvier, 1991, 177-86.

Index

Addis, Robert L.   82
Adorno, Theodor   156, 185
Akselrad, Richard   141n, 157, 179
Alexander, Edward   7, 15, 15n, 20, 32, 33, 52, 59, 115, 132, 179, 188
Amicone, Eddie Eugene   7, 29, 40, 51, 114, 118, 134-135, 189
Andrew, Flynn   135n
Anger, Bert W.   47, 47n, 48, 49, 59n, 81, 121, 124, 134, 136, 143, 150, 152, 188, 189
Arab, Michael   72
Arendt, Hannah   156
Asti, Robert   30, 134
Atlas, Louis   130, 176n
August Wilhelm ["Auwi"]   178, 179n
Aumont, Jean-Pierre   11

Babin, Gary   97
Banfield, Charles M.   13
Bardgett, Edward   100
Bardos, Arthur A.   6, 97, 187, 188, 189
Barr, Robert   143
Barricelli, John P.   43
Beethoven, Ludwig van   179
Behr, Alexandre   97
Békessey, Janos – SEE Habe, Hans
Bernbaum, Robert G. [Glenn]   5
Biberfeld, Ernest S.   97, 141n, 157
Billy, John A.   67
Bond, Jules J.   5, 82
Bourke-White, Margaret   154
Bradley, Omar   49n, 53, 91, 154
Brand, Otto   176n
Brand, Paul Joachim   97
Brecht, Bertolt   156

Brett, Roger   82
Breuer, Robert   36, 82
Broch, Hermann   156
Bultmann, Rudolf   182
Burger, Hanuš [Hans Herbert]   6, 12, 12n, 26, 26n, 40, 41, 49, 50, 51, 52, 53, 60, 66, 67, 79, 80, 88, 89, 98, 102, 158, 159, 160, 160n, 186, 189, 190

Casiero, Michael M.   5
Caskey, Edward A.   10, 132n
Cassini, Igor   6, 16, 21, 21n, 34, 39, 87, 97, 99, 144, 145, 188
Cassini, Marguerite   34
Cassini, Oleg   34
Chopin, Frédéric   179
Churchill, Winston   160
Collette, Jack Travis   135
Collier, Ralph   5
Cook, Rudy   107
Craft, Ray K.   76
Cramer, Ernst   6, 126, 147 148, 153, 154, 169, 170, 173, 180, 190, 191
Cramer, Erwin   169
Cronyn, Hume   11

Dale, Leon Andrew – SEE Dreyfus, Leon Adolphe
Davies, Joseph   11
De Gaulle, Charles   63, 72, 80
Deku, Henry   147, 188
Dekuczynski, Heinz – SEE Deku, Henry
de Milhau, Louis   39, 97
Dentler, Kathryn   35, 36
Deppisch, Hans Curt   59, 59n, 71, 103, 189

Dicks, Henry V.   46, 46n, 47
Dietrich, Josef ["Sepp"]   85, 85n
Ding-Schuler, Erwin   157
Dolan, Patrick   79, 89
Dole, Olcott   142
Donovan, William J. ["Wild Bill"]   10, 48
Doran, Charles   120
Downs, William Randall "Bill"   143
Dreyfus, Leon Adolphe   69, 69n
Dupong, Pierre   93

Eaton, Joseph [Josef Wechsler]   6, 82, 82n, 127, 130, 176 183, 183n, 189
Edel, Leon   6, 17, 17n, 21, 30, 37, 80, 189
Edelman, Daniel   5
Edwards, Ralph   188
Eisenhower, Dwight David   11, 44, 50, 91, 154, 155, 157, 160, 183, 184
Elster, Botho Henning von   131
Enger, Gunther   113
Epstein, Hans J.   5
Eyler, Gordon   104

Fialkoff, Leo D.   141n
Fish, Douglas G.
Flieg, Helmut – SEE Heym, Stefan
Frank, Allesandro   88
Frank, Benno D.   71, 73, 73n, 74, 75, 76, 88, 89, 91, 92, 93, 112, 180. 187, 188
Frick, Gordon M.   32, 33, 50, 187
Frick, Jacob   33
Frick, Wilhelm   187
Frings, Josef   179
Fruendt, Roderick   176n
Furtwängler, Wilhelm   180, 180n

Gatzke, Hans Wilhelm   5
Gieseking, Walter   179, 180, 180n
Gilliland, Ann   34
Goebbels, Joseph   143, 180
Goering, Hermann   187

Goethe, Johann Wolfgang von   156
Goldschlag, Stella   171, 172, 173
Goularte, Joseph C.   36, 82, 187
Grabove, Maxwell   66, 68, 131, 187
Gross, Daniel   193
Guerard, Albert J.   6, 15, 15n, 17, 30, 31, 41, 51, 63, 64, 78, 189, 190
Gunther, Paul F.   97

Habe, Anthony Niklas   11
Habe, Eleanor – SEE Hutton, Eleanor Post
Habe, Hans [Janos Békessey]   6, 11, 12, 13, 14, 17, 18, 19, 20, 20n, 21, 22, 23, 24, 25, 26 27, 28, 31, 37, 39, 42n, 46, 47, 78 79, 80, 82, 85, 86, 88, 93, 96, 97, 130, 171, 175, 176, 177, 183, 184, 185, 185n, 186, 189, 190
Hadley, Arthur T.   6, 37, 37n, 39, 50, 70, 132, 133, 134, 137, 138, 139, 140, 147, 148, 187
Hanser, Richard F.   84n
Hart, Peter   97
Hauptmann, Gerhart   180
Heidegger, Martin   156
Heine, Heinrich   60, 62
Hell, Rudolph   132n
Hemingway, Ernest   78
Henschel, Walter   88
Hertz, David   73, 75, 76, 112
Hess, Rudolf   180
Heym, Stefan [Helmut Flieg]   6. 16, 17, 20, 20n, 22, 28, 30, 31, 36, 37, 40, 41, 49, 51, 53, 54, 62, 63, 76, 77, 78, 79n, 82, 84, 84n, 88, 111, 130, 153, 154, 161, 167, 168, 176, 184, 186, 189, 190
Hildesheim, Wolfgang   185
Hitler, Adolf   38, 83, 84, 90, 136, 156, 172, 178, 179, 180, 181, 183, 186, 190
Hoag, Kenneth C.   5
Hodges, Courtney   49n
Holbert, George   72
Holst, Gustav   82

Hopf, Fridolin   75, 76
Horkheimer, Max   156
Howe, Bertha Josephine   35
Huot, Louis   132n
Hutton, Eleanor Post   11, 79

Inger, Manfred – SEE Lorenz, Fred

Jacobs, Harry   7, 14n
Jaffe, Arthur H.   6, 7, 17, 18n, 29, 30, 31, 33, 58, 63, 66, 67, 71, 73, 75, 106, 131, 132, 134, 187
James, Henry   17
Jarecki, John T.   17, 18n, 36
Jeannotte, Albert   72
Jellin, Curt   6, 88, 154, 168, 169
Jirka   67
Johnson, Lyndon   188
Josselson, Michael   5, 141n
Joyce, William   81, 81n

Kaltenbrunner, Ernst   187
Kant, Immanuel   156
Kästner, Erich   184
Katzenellenbogen, Konrad – SEE Kellen, Konrad
Kellen, Konrad [Katzenellenbogen]   27, 130, 176, 187
Kelly, Gene   11
Kerr, Alfred   185
Kimenthal, Max M.   141n, 157
Klein, Herbert   141
Knoll, Samson B.   6, 49, 52, 53, 60, 61, 62, 81, 128, 148, 181, 185, 189
Koenig, Marie-Pierre   72
Kogon, Eugen   156, 157, 158
Kohner, Hanna Bloch   166, 188
Kohner, Walter   6, 16, 28, 28n, 29, 30, 36, 82, 85, 87, 88, 93, 97, 165, 166, 167, 188
Koplowitz, Oskar – SEE Seidlin, Oskar
Kosse, Gunter   6, 7, 13, 13n, 14, 32, 44, 68, 95, 140, 141, 141n, 187, 189

Kraus, Max W.   5, 6, 176, 177, 185, 188, 189
Kremenliev, Boris 16, 64, 187, 189

Lajoie, Roger A.   5
Langelaan, George   49, 78
Lasky, Abram V. [Victor]   5, 97
Leclerc, Jacques   79
Lehman, Emil   5
Lehr, Owen   178
Leveille, Charles   135
Lewen, Si [Simon Lewin]   6, 7, 18, 18n, 30, 47, 48, 51, 52, 54, 55n, 57, 58, 59, 72, 103, 149, 150, 153, 188, 190
Lewin, Simon – SEE Lewen, Si
Ley, Robert   180
Lincoln, Abraham   190
Lisiecki, Stephen   69
Littman, Edward Hans   187, 187n
Locke, William   100
Loewenbein, Ernest   82, 87
Logan, Max   97
Longley, Henry   142
"Lord Hee-Haw" – SEE Joyce, William
Lorenz, Fred [Manfred Inger]   16, 16n, 73, 73n, 74, 88, 112, 187, 190
Lorre, Peter   11
Louis, Joe   41

MacArthur, Douglas   22
Macon, Robert C.   131
Mann, Heinrich   185
Mann, Thomas   185
Marcuse, Herbert   156
Margaret of Hessen.....   178n
Martin, Marco   190
Maxted, Stanley   119, 143
McClure, Robert A.   82, 175
Meade, George Gordon   13
Meier, Adolph E.   97
Mellitz, Louis   100
Mendelssohn, Felix   62, 179, 180
Messinger, Fred   69

Metcalf, Thomas   100
Mickey, Irving B.   69
Morgan, Brewster   92
Moskovits, Rudolf   107
Mountbatten, Louis   178
Muhlbauer, Louis C.   119, 143, 178
Murrow, Edward R.   143

Niemöller, Martin   63, 183, 185

O'Neill, Con   10
Orbaan, Albert F.   5, 97
Orff, Carl   180
Overton, Daniel   71, 110

Paley, William S.   82
Patton, George   22, 49n, 154
Paul, Frieda   182
Paul, Fritz   182
Pender, Gaston Lewis   33, 35, 36, 117, 139, 140, 188, 189
Pender, William Dorsey   33, 36
Perkins, Francis D.   5, 97
Perutz, Fred W.   6, 7, 15, 15n, 35, 82, 86, 97, 125, 166, 167, 188
Perutz, Margaret   35
Phillian, Sarkis [or Philian]   5, 100
Pines, Philip [Pinkofsky]   7, 15, 15n, 32, 42, 45, 51, 53, 65, 71, 72, 119, 132, 142, 143, 178, 188, 189
Pinkofsky, Philip – SEE Pines, Philip
Powell, Clifford R.   49, 76, 158, 175
Powhatan, Talmadge Huey   69
Preston, Lieutenant   140

Rapoport, Emanuel   140
Reichenbach, Walter   113
Ribbentrop, Joachim von   180
Rinser, Luise   185
Roosevelt, Eleanor   11
Roosevelt, Franklin Delano   9n, 10
Rosenbaum, Sam   81

Rosenberg, Albert G.   6, 7, 14, 14n, 23, 39, 97, 122, 136, 137, 141, 148, 149, 154, 155, 156, 157, 158, 158n, 170, 171, 178, 179, 182, 188, 189
Rotterman, Eugene A., Jr.   71
Ruff, Leopold   43
Ruth, George Herman ("Babe")   87

Sailer, William   81
Saint, Eva Marie   35
Salvatori, Albert H.   64, 132n
Sammaripa, Alexis   137
Sampson, Alfred H.   141n, 157
Sandburg, Carl   185n
Sauckel, Fritz   143n, 187
Schlesinger, Herbert   97
Schirach, Baldur von   157
Schoeppler, Otto, Jr.   7, 20, 35, 35n, 46, 47, 48, 49, 59n, 71, 102, 120, 136, 150, 152, 188, 189, 190
Schumann, Robert   179
Seemann, Clarence ("Ace")   35, 188
Segal, Robert   102
Seidlin, Oskar [Koplowitz]   51, 51n, 160, 189
Seitz, Gene   100
Semprún, Jorge   155, 155n, 156
Sharpe, George H.   13
Shils, Edward   47
Shives, Clyde E.   6, 30, 48, 48n, 133, 189
Shostakovich, Dmitri   41
Simon, John   97
Simpson, William H.   49n
Smith, Howard K.   143
Speyer, Gerhard   176n
Stalin, Joseph   160
Steinberg (cook)   33
Steinberg, Bert   141
Stern, Milton R.   6, 33, 189
Stohr, Albert   179
Straus, Oskar   135
Straus, Walter   135, 136
Strauss, Erwin   176n
Strauss, Richard   180

Strobl, Anthon J., Jr. [Tony]   16, 189

Tennenbaum, Jacob   50, 58
Theriault, Elmer J.   97
Tierney, Gene   34
Toombs, Alfred   89
Truman, Harry S.   160

Vagts, Erich   182
Vogel, Arthur   64

Wagner, Richard   91
Wallenberg, Hans   186, 186n
Warren, Russel   100
Watts, Imlay   110
Wechsberg, Joseph   16, 82, 97, 163, 164, 165, 166, 167, 176, 190

Weidenreich, Peter H. – SEE Wyden, Peter
Wilder, Billy   159, 160, 160n
Wilmott, Chester   143
Wilson, Raymond   131
Windsor, William   101
Wittler, Kurt   176n
Wolf, Tom   69
Woller, Roland G.   141n
Wyden, Peter H.   6, 21, 21n, 41, 51, 82, 84n, 130, 131, 171, 172, 173, 176, 189
Wynder, Ernst   130, 176n, 189

Ziffer, Ewald   35
Ziffer, Sylvia   35